THE MILITARY AND
AMERICAN SOCIETY

The Insight Series

Studies in Contemporary Issues

from Glencoe Press

Series Editors: Fred Krinsky and Joseph Boskin

THE MILITARY AND AMERICAN SOCIETY

Martin B. Hickman
Professor of Political Science
Brigham Young University

GLENCOE PRESS
A Division of The Macmillan Company
Beverly Hills, California
Collier-Macmillian Ltd., London

GLENCOE PRESS
A Division of The Macmillan Company
8701 Wilshire Boulevard
Beverly Hills, California 90211
Collier-Macmillan Canada, Ltd., Toronto, Canada

Library of Congress catalog number: 73-153659

First Printing 1971

Contents

THE MILITARY AND
AMERICAN SOCIETY

Chapter One

The Military and Society

Militarism has been, from the beginning of the Republic, a "dirty" word in the lexicon of American political rhetoric. The complaints of the American colonists in the Declaration of Independence that the King, "has kept among us in, time of peace, Standing Armies without the Consent of our legislature," and that "he has affected to render the Military independent of and superior to the Civil power" have echoed throughout the course of American history. They were reflected in the scorn which Americans heaped upon the "militaristic" societies of Germany and Japan in World War II. Yet this mistrust of standing armies and militarism has been matched by a warm affection for military heroes and praise for feats of valor and bravery in war. This curious ambivalence reflects the basic dualism which has characterized American attitudes toward the military. This dualism rests on a sharp distinction between peace and war. In times of peace, military skills are not relevant to the problems of American life except in protecting the frontier. Therefore, in foreign and domestic affairs the military has had little voice. Symbolic of this exclusion of the military from policy questions during times of peace was the reaction of Secretary of State William Jennings Bryan to suggested civilian military consultations early in Woodrow Wilson's first administration: "He (Bryan) thundered out that army and navy officers could not be trusted to say what we should and should not do, till we actually got into war; that we were discussing how to wage war, but how not to get into war."*

Simultaneously, this dualism has been reflected in a certain scorn for military life. A professional military career has not been highly prized, and American youth has been urged to choose careers in other professions, business, and education. As late as 1955, the prestige of the officer in the armed services was ranked in public opinion polls below that of physician, scientist, college professor, minister, and public school teacher. †

In times of war, the reverse has taken place. Great value has been placed on military skills and professional military leaders. The fullest expression of this military ascendency occurred in World War II. Historians of the war almost uniformly note the importance of Marshall, Eisenhower, King, and the other American military leaders in determining American diplomatic and military strategy during the war. They further assert that this influence led to the subordination of political issues to the demands of military strategy. The classic case was General Eisenhower's decision not to push for the capture of Berlin because it was not a vital military objective. Moreover, in contrast to past wars where, with the exception of General Scott, Admiral Dewey, and General Pershing, the heroes had been citizen soldiers such as Washington, Grant, Lee, Teddy Roosevelt, and Jackson, in World War II the heroes were professional soldiers — Eisenhower, Marshall, Patton, King, Nimitz, Arnold, Bradley, and Halsey.

The dualistic approach to military life characteristic of the United States before 1940 was sharply modified during World War II. After the victory over the Axis, the technological revolution heralded by the atomic bomb and the emergence of the United States as a world power have obscured even further the line between war and peace on which the traditional dualism rested. Instead, Americans have come to believe in the necessity of integrating the military into all aspects of foreign policy planning. There has been a complete rejection of

---

* Quoted in Ernest R. May's, "The Development of Political Military Consultation in the United States," *An American Foreign Policy Reader*, ed. Harry Howe Ranson, (New York: Thomas Y. Crowell, 1969), p. 132.

† Morris Janowitz, *The Professional Soldier*, (Glencoe, Ill: Free Press, 1960), p. 4.

Secretary Bryan's suspicion of the military and a warm embrace of the virtues of military-civilian cooperation. The Vietnamese war has raised the question of whether or not the reaction against the traditional dualism has taken us too far toward the other extreme, military domination of American life. That is the central question in the selections that follow. General Shoup and Professor Fleming argue the affirmative; William Leavitt and Anthony Hartley raise objection to that thesis; and Professor Hillam shows how a foreign policy involving a selective use of force rapidly becomes for the military an end rather than a means. Finally, in what is surely to become a controversial article, Professor McClelland proposes expanding the role of the military in the management of internal conflict.

The New American Militarism*

General David M. Shoup

General David M. Shoup, a hero of the Battle of Tarawa in 1943, served as Commandant of the United States Marine Corps for four years until his retirement in December, 1963.

America has become a militaristic and aggressive nation. Our massive and swift invasion of the Dominican Republic in 1965, concurrent with the rapid buildup of U.S. military power in Vietnam, constituted an impressive demonstration of America's readiness to execute military contingency plans and to seek military solutions to problems of political disorder and potential Communist threats in the areas of our interest.

This "military task force" type of diplomacy is in the tradition of our more primitive, pre-World War II "gunboat diplomacy," in which we landed small forces of Marines to protect

---

* General David M. Shoup, "The New American Militarism," *The Atlantic Monthly*, 223 (April 1969), p. 53.

American lives and property from the perils of native bandits and revolutionaries. In those days the U.S. Navy and its Marine landing forces were our chief means, short of war, for showing the flag, exercising American power, and protecting U.S. interests abroad. The Navy, enjoying the freedom of the seas, was a visible and effective representative of the nation's sovereign power. The Marines could be employed ashore "on such other duties as the President might direct" without congressional approval or a declaration of war. The U.S. Army was not then used so freely because it was rarely ready for expeditionary service without some degree of mobilization, and its use overseas normally required a declaration of emergency or war. Now, however, we have numerous contingency plans involving large joint Air Force-Army-Navy-Marine task forces to defend U.S. interests and to safeguard our allies wherever and whenever we suspect Communist aggresssion. We maintain more than 1,517,000 American in uniform overseas in 119 countries. We have 8 treaties to help defend 48 nations if they ask us to—or if we choose to intervene in their affairs. We have an immense and expensive military establishment, fueled by a gigantic defense industry, and millions of proud, patriotic, and frequently bellicose and militaristic citizens. How did this militarist culture evolve? How did this militiarism steer us into the tragic military and political morass of Vietnam?

Prior to World War II, American attitudes were typically isolationist, pacifist, and generally anti-military. The regular peacetime military establishment enjoyed small prestige and limited influence upon national affairs. The public knew little about the armed forces, and only a few thousand men were attracted to military service and careers. In 1940 there were but 428,000 officers and enlisted men in the Army and Navy. The scale of the war, and the world's power relationships which resulted, created the American military giant. Today the active armed forces contain over 3.4 million men and women, with an additional 1.6 million ready reserves and National Guardsmen.

America's vastly expanded world role after World War II hinged upon military power. The voice and views of the professional military people became increasingly prominent. During the postwar period, distinguished military leaders from the war years filled many top positions in government. Generals

Marshall, Eisenhower, MacArthur, Taylor, Ridgway, LeMay, and others were not only popular heroes but respected opinion-makers. It was a time of international readjustment; military minds offered the benefit of firm views and problem-solving experience to the management of the nation's affairs. Military procedures—including the general staff system, briefings, estimates of the situation, and the organizational and operational techniques of the highly schooled, confident military professionals—spread throughout American culture.

World War II had been a long war. Millions of young American men had matured, been educated, and gained rank and stature during their years in uniform. In spite of themselves, many returned to civilian life as indoctrinated, combat-experienced military professionals. They were veterans, and for better or worse would never be the same again. America will never be the same either. We are now a nation of veterans. To the 14.9 million veterans of World War II, Korea added another 5.7 million five years later, and ever since, the large peacetime military establishment has been training and releasing draftees, enlistees, and short-term reservists by the hundreds of thousands each year. In 1968 the total living veterans of U.S. military service numbered over 23 million, or about 20 percent of the adult population.

Today most middle-aged men, most business, government, civic, and professional leaders, have served some time in uniform. Whether they liked it or not, their military training and experience have affected them, for the creeds and attitudes of the armed forces are powerful medicine, and can become habit-forming. The military codes include all the virtues and beliefs used to motivate men of high principle: patriotism, duty and service to country, honor among fellowmen, courage in the face of danger, loyalty to organization and leaders, self-sacrifice for comrades, leadership, discipline, and physical fitness. For many veterans the military's efforts to train and indoctrinate them may well be the most impressive and influential experience they have ever had—especially so for the young and less educated.

In addition, each of the armed forces has its own special doctrinal beliefs and well-catalogued customs, traditions, rituals, and folklore upon which it strives to build a fiercely loyal military character and esprit de corps. All ranks are taught that their unit and their branch of the military service are the most elite, important, efficient, or effective in the military establishment. By believing in the superiority and importance of their own service they also provide themselves a degree of personal status, pride, and self-confidence.

As they get older, many veterans seem to romanticize and exaggerate their own military experience and loyalties. The policies, attitudes, and positions of the powerful veterans' organizations such as the American Legion, Veterans of Foreign Wars, and AMVETS, totaling over 4 million men, frequently reflect this pugnacious and chauvinistic tendency. Their memberships generally favor military solutions to world problems in the pattern of their own earlier experience, and often assert that their military service and sacrifice should be repeated by the younger generations.

Closely related to the attitudes and influence of America's millions of veterans is the vast and powerful complex of the defense industries, which have been described in detail many times in the eight years since General Eisenhower first warned of the military-industrial power complex in his farewell address as President. The relationship between the defense industry and the military establishment is closer than many citizens realize. Together they form a powerful public opinion lobby. The several military service associations provide both a forum and a meeting ground for the military and its industries. The associations also provide each of the armed services with a means of fostering their respective roles, objectives, and propaganda.

Each of the four services has its own association, and there are also additional military function associations, for ordinance, management, defense industry, and defense transportation, to name some of the more prominent. The Air Force Association and the Association of the U.S. Army are the largest, best organized, and most effective of the service associations. The Navy League, typical of the "silent service" traditions, is not as well coordinated in its public relations efforts, and the small Marine Corps Association is not even in the same arena with the other contenders, the Marine Association's main activity being the publication of a semi-officially monthly magazine. Actually, the service associations' respective magazines, with an estimated combined circulation of over 270,000, are the primary medium serving the several associations' purposes . . .

The American people have also become more and more accustomed to militarism, to uniforms, to the cult of the gun, and to the violence of combat. Whole generations have been brought up on war news and wartime propaganda; the few years of peace since 1939 have seen a steady stream of war novels, war movies, comic strips, and television programs with war or military settings. To many Americans, military training, expeditionary service, and warfare are merely extensions of the entertainment and games of childhood. Even the weaponry and hardware they use at war are similar to the highly realistic toys of their youth. Soldiering loses appeal for some of the relatively few who experience the blood, terror, and filth of battle; for many, however, including far too many senior professional officers, war and combat are an exciting adventure, a competitive game, and an escape from the dull routines of peacetime.

It is this influential nucleus of aggressive, ambitious professional military leaders who are the root of America's evolving militarism. There are over 410,000 commissioned officers on active duty in the four armed services. Of these, well over half are junior ranking reserve officers on temporary active duty. Of the 150,000 or so regular career officers, only a portion are senior ranking colonels, generals, and admirals, but it is they who constitute the elite core of the military establishment. It is these few thousand top-ranking professionals who command and manage the armed forces and plan and formulate military policy and opinion. How is it, then, that in spite of civilian controls and the national desire for peace, this small group of men exert so much martial influence upon the government and life of the American people?

The military will disclaim any excess of power or influence on their part. They will point to their small numbers, low pay, and subordination to civilian masters as proof of their modest status and innocence. Nevertheless, the professional military, as a group, is probably one of the best organized and most influential of the various segments of the American scene. Three wars and six major contingencies since 1940 have forced the Amercian people to become abnormally aware of the armed forces and their leaders. In turn the military services have produced an unending supply of distinguished, capable, articulate, and effective leaders. The sheer skill, energy, and dedication of America's military officers make them dominant in almost every government or civic organization they may inhabit, from the federal Cabinet to the local PTA.

The hard core of high-ranking professionals are, first of all, mostly service academy graduates: they had to be physically and intellectually above average among their peers just to gain entrance to an academy. Thereafter for the rest of their careers they are exposed to constant competition for selection and promotion. Attrition is high, and only the most capable survive to reach the elite senior ranks. Few other professions have such rigorous selection systems; as a result, the top military leaders are top-caliber men . . .

In general the military are better organized, they work harder, they think straighter, and they keep their eyes on the objective, which is to be instantly ready to solve the problem through military action while ensuring that their respective service gets its proper mission, role, and recognition in the operation. In an emergency the military usually have a ready plan; if not, their numerous doctrinal manuals provide firm guidelines for action. Politicians, civilian appointees, and diplomats do not normally have the same confidence about how to react to threats and violence as do the military.

The motivations behind these endeavors are difficult for civilians to understand. For example, military professionals cannot measure the success of their individual efforts in terms of personal financial gain. The armed forces are not profit-making organizations, and the rewards for excellence in the military profession are acquired in less tangible forms. Thus it is that promotion and the responsibilities of higher command, with the related fringe benefits of quarters, servants, privileges, and prestige, motivate most career officers. Promotions and choice job opportunities are attained by constantly performing well, conforming to the expected patterns, and pleasing the senior officers. Promotions and awards also frequently result from heroic and distinguished performance in combat, and it takes a war to become a military hero. Civilians can scarcely understand or even believe that many ambitious military professionals truly yearn for wars and the opportunities for glory and distinction afforded only in combat. A career of peacetime duty is a dull and frustrating prospect for the normal regular officer to contemplate.

The professional military leaders of the U.S. Armed Forces have some additional motivations which influence their readiness to involve their country in military ventures. Unlike some of the civilian policy-makers, the military has not been obsessed with the threat of Communism per se. Most military people know very little about Communism either as a doctrine or as a form of government. But they have been given reason enough to presume that it is bad and represents the force of evil. When they can identify "Communist aggression," however, the matter then becomes of direct concern to the armed forces. Aggressors are the enemy in the war games, the "bad guys," the "Reds." Defeating aggression is a gigantic combat-area competition rather than a crusade to save the world from Communism. In the military view, all "Communist aggression" is certain to be interpreted as a threat to the United States.

The armed forces' role in performing its part of the national security policy—in addition to defense against actual direct attack on the United States and to maintaining the strategic atomic deterrent forces—is to be prepared to employ its *General Purpose Forces* in support of our collective security policy and the related treaties and alliances. To do this it deploys certain forces to forward zones in the Unified Commands, and maintains an up-to-date file of scores of detailed contingency plans which have been thrashed out and approved by the Joint Chiefs of Staff. Important features of these are the movement or deployment schedules of task forces assigned to each plan. The various details of these plans continue to create intense rivalries between the Navy-Marine sealift forces and the Army-Air Force team of air-mobility proponents. At the senior command levels parochial pride in service, personal ambitions, and old Army-Navy gave rivalry stemming back to academy loyalties can influence strategic planning far more than most civilians would care to believe. The game is to be ready for deployment sooner than the other elements of the joint task force and to be so disposed as to be the first to fight. The danger presented by this practice is that readiness and deployment speed become ends in themselves. This was clearly revealed in the massive and rapid intervention in the Dominican Republic in 1965 when the contingency plans and interservice rivalry appeared to supersede diplomacy. Before the world realized what was happening, the momentum and velocity of the military plans propelled almost 20,000 U.S. soldiers and Marines into the small turbulent republic in an impressive race to test the respective mobility of the Army and the Marines, and to attain overall command of U.S. Forces Dom. Rep. Only a fraction of the force deployed was needed or justified. A small 1935-model Marine landing force could probably have handled the situation. But the Army airlifted much of the 82nd Airborne Division to the scene, including a lieutenant general, and took charge of the operation.

Simultaneously, in Vietnam during 1965 the four services were racing to build up combat strength in that hapless country. This effort was ostensibly to save South Vietnam from Viet Cong and North Vietnamese aggression. It should also be noted that it was motivated in part by the same old interservice rivalry to demonstrate respective importance and combat effectiveness.

The punitive air strikes immediately following the Tonkin Gulf incident in late 1964 revealed the readiness of naval air forces to bomb North Vietnam. (It now appears that the Navy actually had attack plans ready even before the alleged incident took place!) So by early 1965 the Navy carrier people and the Air Force initiated a contest of comparative strikes, sorties, tonnages dropped, "Killed by Air" claims, and target grabbing which continued up to the 1968 bombing pause. Much of the reporting on air action has consisted of misleading data or propaganda to serve Air Force and Navy purposes. In fact, it became increasingly apparent that the U.S. bombing effort in both North and South Vietnam has been one of the most wasteful and expensive hoaxes ever to be put over on the American people. Tactical and close air support of ground operations is essential, but air power use in general has to a large degree been a contest for the operations planners, "fine experience" for young pilots, and opportunity for career officers.

The highly trained professional and aggressive career officers of the Army and Marine Corps played a similar game. Prior to the decision to send combat units to South Vietnam in early 1965, both services were striving to increase their involvement. The Army already had over 16,000 military aid personnel serving in South Vietnam in the military adviser role, in training missions, logistic services, supporting heliocopter companies, and in Special Forces teams. This investment of men and matériel justified a requirement for additional U.S. combat units to provide local security and to help protect our growing commitment of aid to the South Vietnam regime.

There were also top-ranking Army officers who wanted to project Army ground combat units into the Vietnam struggle for a variety of other reasons; to test plans and new equipment, to test the new air-mobile theories and tactics, to try the tactics and techniques of counter-insurgence, and to gain combat experience for young officers and noncommissioned officers. It also appeared to be a case of the military's duty to stop "Communist aggression" in Vietnam ...

For years up to 1964 the chiefs of the armed services, of whom the author was then one, deemed it unnecessary and unwise for U.S. forces to become involved in any ground war in Southeast Asia. In 1964 there were changes in the composition of the Joint Chiefs of Staff, and in a matter of a few months the Johnson Administration, encouraged by the aggressive miliary, hastened into what has become the quagmire of Vietnam. The intention at the time was that the war effort be kept small and "limited." But as the momentum and involvement built up, the military leaders rationalized a case that this was not a limited-objective exercise, but was a proper war in defense of the United States against "Communist agression" and in honor of our area commitments ...

Some of the credibility difficulties experienced by the Johnson Administration over its war situation reports and Vietnam policy can also be blamed in part upon the military advisers. By its very nature most military activity falls under various degrees of security classification. Much that the military plans or does must be kept from the enemy. Thus the military is indoctrinated to be secretive, devious, and misleading in its plans and operations. It does not, however, always confine its security restrictions to purely military operations. Each of the services and all of the major commands practice techniques of controlling the news and the release of self-serving propaganda: in "the interests of national defense," to make the service look good, to cover up mistakes, to build up and publicize a distinguished military personality, or to win a round in the continuous gamesmanship of the interservice contest. If the Johnson Administration suffered from lack of credibility in its reporting of the war, the truth would reveal that much of the hocus-pocus stemmed from schemers in the military services, both at home and abroad.

Our militaristic culture was born of the necessities of World War II, nurtured by the Korean War, and became an accepted aspect of American life during the years of cold war emergencies and real or imagined threats from the Communist bloc. Both the philosophy and the institutions of militarism grew during these years because of the momentum of their own dynamism, the vigor of their ideas, their large size and scope, and because of the dedicated concentration of the emergent military leaders upon their doctrinal objectives. The dynamism of the defense establishment and its culture is also inspired and stimulated by vast amounts of money, by the new creations of military research and materiel development, and by the concepts of the Defense Department-supported "think factories." These latter are extravagantly funded civilian organizations of scientists, analysts, and retired military strategists who feed new militaristic philosophies into the Defense Department to help broaden the views of the single service doctrinaires, to create fresh policies and new requirements for ever larger, more expensive defense forces.

Somewhat like a religion, the basic appeals of anti-Communism, national defense, and patriotism provide the foundation for a powerful creed upon which the defense establishment can build, grow, and justify its cost. More so than many large bureaucratic organizations, the defense establishment now devotes a large share of its efforts to self-perpetuation, to justifying its organizations, to preaching its doctrines and to self-maintenance and management. Warfare becomes an extension of war games and field test. War justifies the existence of the establishment, provides experience for the military novice and challenge for the senior officer. Wars and emergencies put the military and their leaders on the front pages and give status and prestige to the professionals. Wars add to the military traditions, the self-nourishment of heroic deeds, and provide a new crop of military leaders who become the rededicated disciples of the code of service and military action. Being recognized public figures in a nation always seeking folk heroes, the military leaders have been largely exempt from the criticism experienced by the more plebeian politician. Flag officers are considered "experts," and their views are often accepted by press and Congress as the gospel. In turn, the distinguished military leader feels obligated not only to perpetuate loyally the doctrine of his service but to comply with the stereotyped military characteristics by being tough, aggressive, and firm in his resistance to Communist aggression and his belief in the military solutions to world problems. Standing closely behind these leaders, encouraging and prompting them, are the rich and powerful defense industries. Standing in front, adorned with service caps, ribbons, and lapel emblems, is a nation of veterans — patriotic, belligerent, romantic, and well intentioned, finding a certain sublimation and excitement in their country's latest military venture. Militarisms in America is in full bloom and promises a future of vigorous self-pollination — unless the blight of Vietnam reveals that militarism is more a poisonous weed than a glorious blossom.

(NOTE. — *The opinions contained herein are the private ones of the author and are not to be construed as official or reflecting the views of the Navy Department or the naval service at large.*)

Will Militarism Destroy the United States?*

D. F. Fleming

* D. F. Fleming, "Will Militarism Destroy the United States?," *Foreign Military Commitments: The Forensic Quarterly*, 43 (November 1969). Copyright 1969. Reprinted by permission.

Mr. Fleming, Emeritus Professor of International Relations at Vanderbilt University, is the author of the two-volume work, *The Cold War and Its Origins, 1917-1960*, now in its fifth printing. Another book, *America's Role in Asia*, is currently in press.

A large, inflexible military organization unchecked by strong civilian review can lead only to a self-perpetuating drain on national treasure, a demoralized citizenry, and foreign policies dangerously irrelevant in a world moving rapidly away from traditional forms of war and diplomacy. — Wall Street Journal editorial, March 19, 1969.

It is an almost unbelievable fact that the United States has become the greatest military power that has ever existed on earth, and that its military machine not only considers the world to be its province, but incidentally dominates the internal life of the country. It is also a power so vast that it may be impossible ever to curb or reduce it.

As one who grew up in the period of our carefree isolationism before 1914, I should hasten to explain that the great military machines of Europe suddenly clashed in World War I, and that a new weapon, the German submarine, eventually drew us into that war to defend our rights on the seas and to ward off the domination of all Europe by German militarism.

The devoted efforts of Woodrow Wilson to end such pitiful tragedies failed. He achieved the League of Nations but the United States refused to lead it, choosing to practice isolationism again until another German effort to conquer all Europe (while Japan tried to subdue the Far East) brought us into the even more destructive World War II of 1939-1945. 1945.

Then the new United Nations was pushed aside by the Cold War with the Truman Doctrine forbidding all future revolutions, lest they might turn Red, and proclaiming the "containment" of both the Soviet Union and Communism everywhere. Very soon the encirclement of China with a vast ring of armed power, close up to her shores, was added. Commitments to defend forty-four states in our world-wide chains of alliances were also reinforced by the desire to protect expanding American investments throughout the entire non-Communist world, giving us a world police role of global proportions.

The Military-Industrial Complex

Naturally this gigantic undertaking entailed enormous armaments and a huge military establishment. In his Farewell Address as President, General Dwight D. Eisenhower warned in 1961 that military establishment and the industry which armed it might come to permeate and control our entire national life, and this has almost happened.

The term military-industrial complex no longer describes the immensity of our submission to militarism. To be sure there is the most intimate tie-up between the great military bureaucracy in the Pentagon and the industrial interests that profit so hugely from the military contracts, but labor union members benefit richly and even the universities get lush research grants from the military, which put many professors aboard the gravy train that is protected by entrenched committee chairmen in both houses of Congress. Eric Sevareid spoke accurately of "the suffocating growth of the military-industrial-academic-labor union-congressional complex" All of these groups and others enjoy the very loosely controlled flow of tax money into their hands. Together they are still a minority of us but a very powerful one.

At the heart of this giant complex are the men who have made the armed forces their life work, especially the officers. General David M. Shoup, a former Commandant of the United States Marine Corps, has described unforgettably the "nucleus of aggressive, ambitious professional military leaders who are the root of America's evolving militarism." He notes that there are "over 410,000 commissioned officers on active duty in the armed services."

Their lives are relatively tame in peacetime, so that during 1965 all "four services were racing to build up strength" in Viet Nam. It is war, adds Sevareid, which gives our officers "their promotions, renown and sense of being usefully alive; no other experience compares with it for the male ego."

These men are carefully selected for ability and even in peacetime, Shoup writes, "The sheer skill, energy, and dedication of America's military officers make them dominant in almost every government or civic organization they may inhabit, from federal Cabinet to the local PTA."

This capacity is reinforced, says Brigadier General (Ret.)

Hugh B. Hester, by an "enormous" propaganda budget in the Defense Department which "covers every segment of our society." All officers "including retired ones, are given prepared speeches to deliver."

Of course the defense budget itself is enormous. The one proposed for 1970 adds up to $78,475,047,000 and Rear Admiral (Ret.) Arnold E. True testified accurately before the Senate Armed Services Committee that "The only real threat to our national security is the existence of huge stockpiles of nuclear weapons in the U.S. and the U.S.S.R. and the smaller stockpiles in China." The motivation for maintaining these stockpiles, he adds, is fear and "as long as these weapons exist, there is no security for the U.S. or the other nations of the world" — a fact never to be forgotten. "Our military establishment itself has grown to such a size that it indicates a national paranoia and it may well be its continued growth will bring on World War III which it is designed to prevent."

This is a strong statement from a man entitled to make it. It is verified in an arresting address by Senator J. William Fulbright in which he shows a "disparity of almost ten to one between federal military expenditures since World War II and regular national budgetary expenditures for education, welfare, health and housing."

"Mad Momentum"

This is obviously the road to national debility and disaster. Yet we are very far advanced on it. Back in September, 1967, Defense Secretary Robert McNamara described the "mad momentum" of the missile arms race. In early 1969, Professor Milton J. Rosenberg, professor of social psychology at the University of Chicago, surveyed most competently our drift toward doomsday. He found it powered by "an essentially paranoid axiom: one must conceive the worst the opposing power *could* do and then operate on the assumption that, if unchecked, it *will* do it." This is an exact statement of the rule we live by and it *is* paranoid. It leaves no room for humanity, for normal human reactions, or for the desire of all peoples to live in peace and enjoy increasingly the fruits of their labors and advancing technologies.

The paranoid axiom is also self-defeating. Rosenberg cites

McNamara's statement made in February, 1965. "At each successively higher level of U.S. expenditures, the ratio of our costs for Damage Limitation to the potential aggressor's costs for Assured Destruction becomes less and less favorable to us." To try to limit our fatalities to about 40 million in a first strike against us "we would have to spend on Damage Limiting programs about four times what the potential aggressor would have to spend on Damage creating forces" — and, he might have added, always sleep in the holes in the ground assigned to the most favored of us.

Rosenberg concluded that, "If the game is madly played on both sides, there is still some special madness in our insistence on staying far ahead of the Communist nations in destructive and 'defensive' capability," and "a special duplicity in the fact that our military manage to find unbearable threats in every attempt by the Soviets or Chinese to narrow the gap between our capabilities and theirs."

Another scholar, Professor Benedict J. Kerkvliet, of the University of Wisconsin, has surveyed the whole notion of defense by nuclear deterrence and has concluded that it would be more prudent to begin unilateral disarmament. The deterrence strategy "seems to be only a rational one for insane societies."

This is an accurate statement when one reflects that there is literally no limit to the deterrence game, short of final national disintegration. Our scientists who are well paid to think up "new weapons systems" can be absolutely depended upon to pile new and ever more expensive systems on top of each other. There is no limit in the sky, where most of them will operate. This is proved by the fantastic purposes and capabilities of the ABM and MIRV systems.

ABM and MIRV

If we have nuclear missiles capable of crossing half the world it is logical to invent Anti Ballistic Missiles (ABMs) to "defend" our cities and missile sites, especially since we already have on our missiles Multiple Re-entry Vehicles (MRVs), each of which can scatter several missiles on the target. Naturally this is not good enough, so we plan MIRVs that can think along the way and then at a thousandth of some second fire missiles at several *different* targets, over a large area. This patently requires super-super ABMs and so on into eternity. No one has yet figured out how to counter the missile firing submarines deep under the sea, but give us triple X billions of dollars and a new spiral to national oblivion, one way or another, will open. By this route there is no escape from our final fiery end.

Nor can this game go on much longer. Indeed, the MIRV decision may be the last stopping place before doomsday: this weapon must be tested often in the sky and nothing can prevent the scientific eyes of our opponents, in earth satellites and otherwise, from seeing the many missiles on the warhead scatter to targets. This will open up "an anti-missile gap in reverse" for both sides. Indeed "the Department of Defense is openly putting high accuracy on the 8,000 additional warheads [on the MIRVs], so that they can be used to attack Soviet land-based missiles."

If the plunge into the ABM-MIRV desperation cycle is not prevented, there will be no stopping place for several years in the insanity of the arms race.

Military Socialism

By any objective standard the American people are on the steep incline of militarism, with the deep waters below them darkened by the ink of many ponderous arms budgets. We proceed downward at an increasing pace also, because the slide is greased by the prodigal use of military socialism.

Welfare socialism—which increases the health, wealth, and productivity of our people—is one thing, but military socialism—which wastes our resources, kills enterprise, and ends in economic sterility—is quite another. The sweet profits and high wages which military spending brings blind many to the fact that the free flowing military dollars create no new wealth, aside from some "spin offs" of military research, and thus end in sterility. Equally destructive also is the side effect of killing enterprise and initiative along the way. Why work hard or save dollars when contracts are let quietly without bidding, when costs of weapons hardware are allowed to rise several hundred per cent without any penalty to the contractors, all at the expense of taxes; when new military gadgets costing billions prove to be partial or total failures, without any penalties or relief to overburdened taxpayers. This kind of socialism, the negation of all private enterprise, must bring the richest of nations to bankruptcy and disintegration. Up to a certain point military priming of the economic pump may seem as good as any, but its negative fruits must eventually exhaust our economic wells.

We cannot be strong by endlessly squandering our wealth on defense when the deep social needs of our people, needs that will not wait much longer, threaten anarchy in cities and nation alike. We were told once that we could afford both unlimited guns and social reforms. Now we know that this is not true. The military costs eat up the social gains, and weaken us daily.

There is only one way that we can be strong and respected in the world, even loved. That is by building here at home such a workable, prosperous, humane society that all the nations will look to us once more as the model to emulate. Moreover, we could then have resources with which to help some of the weaker peoples.

Other Looming Perils

When human pollution of all of our waters, including the oceans, and of our limited supply of air, plus the population explosion, threaten increasingly to end all life on earth, we have no time left for limitless military waste or for phobias about other peoples and their ways of life. With mortal perils like these to face and overcome—if we can—the idea that we are in deadly conflict with Russia or China is "trivial," as George Wald has truly said. The word is shocking, but it is accurate.

We can no longer indulge in the fantasies of the Cold War: that the nearly exhausted Red bear of 1945 would gobble up Western Europe, and that the also victorious Red dragon of 1949 would create havoc in all Asia with its giant tail. Now that Russia and China are almost in a state of war with one another, what requires us to defend all mankind against the two, or either of them?

Professor Fred Warner Neal, of the Claremont Graduate School, has recently pointed out that the claim that the Soviet Union posed "a continuing threat of physical military aggression" against us was always contradicted by Stalin's "inward-looking, defensive, and even isolationist" policies, yet "This assumption about the danger of military aggression from the Communist states has permeated our whole social fabric." We also grasped the illusions "that we could restrain the spread of political doctrine by military means and that revolutions everywhere were Communist inspired and thus constituted a danger to the United States."

Viet Nam Fiasco

These delusions have been exploded by our misadventure in Viet Nam and out of our sad experience there has grown a real hope that our people will curb our militarism.

In Viet Nam our military men and industrial backers have thrown the whole book of military destruction—save only nuclear fire—at a little brown people and have been defeated. The giant B52s have dropped many, many millions of tons of bombs on the peninsula. Countless thousands of times our helicopters have sprayed bullets and napalm, often at night, over the villages and countryside. All kinds of tanks and huge vehicles have thrashed the jungles times without end. The big guns have thundered and the little ones have chattered endlessly. Gas of various kinds has been used.

All this and more has been done and yet the little men who, in the main, fight only with what they can carry, have stymied the military colossus of all time. Our never-ending military effort has divided our nation, brought it to the verge of internal disintegration, driven one President from office, and promises to destroy another. It has aroused a large majority of the people of the world against us and imperiled our prestige with most of the others.

It all came about gradually because the President's military advisers endlessly told him that another dose of force would bring "victory." So the great American eagle is lost in the jungles of Viet Nam and does not know how to escape. Spending $100 billion and nearly 40,000 American lives, while wounding for life perhaps 100,000 others; killing several hundred thousands of natives, mostly innocent people of all ages and both sexes; driving some 3 million more from their homes in the villages to the insecurity and squalor of life in the cities and refugee camps—all this has not given us a sure grip on the so-called strategic spot in South Viet Nam which China allegedly coveted.

This incredible and horrible military failure should teach us a permanent lesson about the nature of power. We thought it resided in the Pentagon, but we have learned that it really lives in the minds and hearts of a small people who are determined to be independent and free of foreign control. It is a thing of the spirit, mightier than all the American swords that seek to find and pierce it.

Pentagon Rule Challenged

If this has not yet been fully understood by our people, the enormity of our military and moral defeat has led a strong minority in Congress to question and oppose the torrents of military money that used to flow through both houses by unanimous votes, or with only one glorious maverick like Senator Wayne Morse or Senator Ernest Gruening voting nay. Now every military item is to be scrutinized, by new devices yet to be perfected. The greatest commentators on television now unite in reporting daily the failures of the garrison state. More than a few leading newspapers now use their great influence in favor of survival as a civilian state.

All this would have been unthinkable two years ago, or even one. Yet this new revulsion may not be strong enough. The Pentagon is the most powerful bureaucracy that ever existed in any land. We fear civilian bureaucracy but have been blind and deaf about the greatest bureauacy of all, the one which extends from the Pentagon out over the American empire to the ends of the earth.

Can Civilian Control Be Effective?

The most important issue in our national life is whether civilian control can ever be made effective again. The very able Defense Secretary McNamara took office "with the avowed aim of establishing greater civilian control over the military," but, according to Richard Goodwin, "the harsh fact . . . is that when he left, the military had greater influence over American policy . . ."

The continuing paramount issue, Goodwin continues, is whether "the Pentagon is to play a fundamental and perhaps mortal role in shaping our national policy, using secret information, building an independent constituency through a vast public relations program, while liberated from the normal restraints of public debate and Congressional judgment."

At the best it will be a long gruelling endeavor, one to enlist the best energies of you young people and your elders. Inexperienced civilian teams move into the Pentagon with each new administration and, among other tough fortresses, they encounter the mightly bastion of secrecy. "The matter is classified. The public must not know. Our national security depends on it!" Yet nearly all information about any question can be obtained by studying the press and other public sources, if people will take the trouble. The need, says former director of the Bureau of the Budget Charles L. Schultze, is for a new joint committee of Congress, properly staffed, and for a multiplicity of independently financed research centers on military affairs in our universities. Behind them must be countless individual citizens who also do their homework on the key issue of our national life, since our survival as a civilian state depends on it.

Until recently, to quote Representative Don Edwards, there has not been "even an effort to have a devil's advocate" against the military. He examined "one series of hearings which ran to 3,000 pages of testimony from 300 witnesses, 298 of whom worked for the Pentagon or within the military services. The other two represented the National Rifle Association. With powerful drives under way to *increase* the military budget in many directions after Viet Nam, opponents of the military state will need all the airs and ideas which can be mustered.

What Ways Out?

What ways are there out of the military morass into which we have partly stumbled and partly blundered deliberately?

These are offered to stimulate other ideas and proposals:

(1) *Our cold war fixations are outdated.* If there was once some partial justification for them, which is debatable, they have been superseded by new and undeniably urgent imperatives. An

increasing number of competent authorities warn us that man's ever greater pollution of our land, water, and air threatens his extinction on this planet in the span of a few decades, and that the geometric rise of population must have the same result in the same short time. Like militarism, these forces may already be beyond control, but we must do what we can, individually and in all kinds of groups. We cannot accept the conclusion that man is doomed by his own follies.

(2) *Militarism is self-destructive.* In the short time that may remain to us as a nation, and as a part of humanity, we must not waste our energies and resources on military socialism. Everything that we have and can create will be imperatively needed to help give mankind a chance at a long tenure on this earth.

(3) *There is no longer any military defense.* The idea that even the greatest "powers" can no longer defend their lands and peoples is deeply shocking, but it is inexorably true. Every unprejudiced person knows it. When the military titans can only die in mutual slaughter involving the sudden death of hundreds of millions, when an accident or a mental aberration in one man may touch off the final deluge of death and when the military acts of a small state may do the same, the very idea of "national defense" is emptied of meaning. Only artificial fears can keep the arms race going until doomsday, and we must be mature enough to refuse to let these fears determine our fate.

(4) *The core interests of the large nations must be mutually respected.* It was a highly dangerous act when we mounted missiles in Italy and Turkey aimed at the Soviet Union, but it was worse folly when years later the Kremlin tried secretly to erect missiles on our very doorstep in Cuba. Yet it is also incredible folly for us to maintain missiles and giant weapons of every kind in a close-up ring around Communist China. That is a sure prescription for a disaster that may involve all mankind.

(5) *We cannot police the world and suppress all revolutions that threaten capitalism and our investments in the non-Communist half of it.* Viet Nam has demonstrated that for all the world to see, and no number of FDLS ships and giant troop-carrying planes can ever restore our fancied world hegemony. When the pressures of population, or pollution, make men

desperate they will revolt, in spite of all engines of death and huge police vehicles that we can fabricate. This means that we cannot enforce *Pax Americana* even in Latin America.

(6) *Neutralization must be pushed.* Many areas of the world, small and large, should be neutralized by the agreement of rival states and others, again narrowing areas of conflict.

(7) *International solutions must be developed rapidly.* This has been the demonstrated, crying need ever since the end of World War I. After it there has never been any other way of escape and this has been more urgently clear during the World War II period and through all the stages of the Cold War. Now time is short, but the United Nations, the World Court, the World Bank and other international institutions still live and their usefulness can be rapidly expanded. It is a hopeful sign that one of the organs of the new administration has recently recommended that our aid to underdeveloped peoples should be channeled through international agencies, with no effort by Americans to profit directly from it.

The term "world government" may still be repellent to many, but nothing less than strong world agencies, open even to Chinese Reds, can hope to cope with the looming dangers that threaten the extinction of all men.

(8) *The young people may save us.* All around the world young people are in revolt. They know well that their fathers and grandfathers have made a dreadful mess of things and they reject the old values: that profit making is the main motive in life; that their function is to obey Communist bureaucracy; and that the Deity ordained that few should live richly while the peoples perish.

Here, then, is a fresh reservoir of hope and action. As you young people begin to move into positions of power and influence, you may provide the stimulus to action for at least the containment of our desperate problems and then for solutions that will give the peoples a chance to live at peace in civilian societies, over a long term.

But time presses more than ever. This writer and many of his generation have worked steadily since 1918 to persuade our countrymen to accept strong international institutions— beginning with the League of Nations—to keep the peace, but without much success.

Now the urgencies are much greater and the time left to us far shorter. You of the younger generation do not have fifty years left in which to labor, and you must have the help of great numbers of your elders, aroused to avert the extinction which hovers over all of us.

Will the Real Dr. Strangelove Please Stand Up?*

William Leavitt

Will the real Dr. Strangelove please stand up? The question is put in all seriousness. It is asked from the point of view of one who views himself as a liberal. It is asked from the point of view of one who is entirely convinced that unless this country focuses its energies on social needs with the same will that has brought us to a manned landing on the moon, we shall be in the kind of trouble that all the technology in the world will not be able to alleviate.

Why put the question? Because now is the time to search for the truth in the national debate over the role of the so-called military-industrial complex in American society. If the truth is drowned in a vortex of hysterical charges, we will not only cripple our ability to influence events in the international area, but also, and even more important, we will succumb to a new virus of McCarthyism. Instead of looking for Communists under every bed, we will be witch-hunting every American in or out of uniform who, regardless of his views on domestic problems believes in the necessity for American strength in a world that continue to be dangerous.

Such a belief in the need for US military strength, it should be pointed out, does not require an accompanying conviction that the Russians or Chinese are ten feet tall and about to attack

* William Leavitt, "Will the Real Dr. Strangelove Please Stand Up?," *Air Force/Space Digest* (July 1969).

us—or, to move to another sphere, to believe that sex education in the schools is some kind of Red plot. Put another way, to believe in the need for US military capabilities to match those of potential enemies does not make the believer a "kook" who would like to see the country converted into a garrison state.

The brand of neo-McCarthyism alluded to is already leading to a tragic polarization of US society. Now, more than any other time in recent history, there is an overriding need for balanced analysis of how we arrived at the distorted debate now being inflicted on the country, in which "the military" is being pilloried, along with its industrial suppliers, for allegedly taking over US foreign policy, generally corrupting American society, distorting national priorities and worst of all dragging the country into an endless, costly, and immoral struggle in Southeast Asia.

The so-called military-industrial complex, we are also told, is attempting to thrust on the country an unworkable and unnecessary anti-missile system, which, if it is deployed, along with new multiwarhead MIRV ICBMs, will destroy for the foreseeable future any real chance for US-Soviet arms-control agreements and will consequently set off an inevitable arms race that may well lead to superpower confrontation and nuclear war. Dr. Strangelove personified. Or so we are told.

Let us explore some of these allegations and examine how we got to where we are now.

Vietnam first. What are we doing there? How did we get into the quagmire? And not incidentally, what are the moral questions that need to be honestly examined?

Was it really the men in uniform and their commanders who are fighting this frustrating war who advocated our involvement in the first place? In the large, the answer is no. Vietnam is primarily the ultimate and sour consequence of policies that evolved in the early 1960s out of disenchantment with the late Secretary of State John Foster Dulles' massive-retaliation policy. Under President Eisenhower and Secretary Dulles, massive retaliation had become the keystone of US strategic policy designed to deter Soviet attacks on the continental US and on Western Europe.

Many advisors to the new Kennedy Administration questioned, and properly so, whether massive retaliation, as devised by Mr. Dulles, had serious credibility shortcomings. Did our NATO allies, and the Soviet Union itself, really believe that the US would risk its national existence by going to nuclear war with Russia to protect Western Europe? Was there not a way, if America had to go to war to meet its pledges to Europe, to keep a US-Russian confrontation non-nuclear?

These were not idle questions. They needed to be asked. But the new men who ruled and influenced the Kennedy/McNamara Pentagon of the early 1960s developed a fascination with what they called limited war. The focus was on Europe at first. And the idea, which excited great enthusiasm, was to reduce the potential horror of war in Europe from nuclear down to conventional terms. The new aim was to develop so-called balanced forces so that we, in concert with what we hoped would be beefed up European conventional forces, could respond to aggression at any level.

It all sounded very neat. We would develop a mix of forces able to handle virtually any kind of threat from nuclear fireball to brushfire war. Students of the period will recall a spate of enthusiasm for conventional war in Europe that seemed to look back upon the unpleasantness of 1939–45 as a veritable garden party. We were even told that the conventional forces of the Soviet Union and its Warsaw Pact allies, in numerical terms, had really been exaggerated and that Western forces were, after all, a good match for the Russians and their satellites, division for division. What happened in Czechoslovakia in 1968 finally shattered that bravado. Or should have.

What began among the Kennedy defense people as a useful critique of massive retaliation and overreliance on strategic nuclear power evolved into a new policy called "flexible response." Its bible was Army General Maxwell Taylor's book *The Uncertain Trumpet,* which brought the General back to prominence in Washington as President Kennedy's military adviser, then Chairman of the Joint Chiefs of Staff, and finally as Ambassador to Saigon. But General Taylor was by no means the only advocate of flexible response. And it ought to be pointed out, for the benefit of those who find it convenient to view "the military" as a monolith, that as limited war came to the dogmatic fore, it was not surprisingly, the Army that most strongly supported the concept. Limited war promised to restore the ground service's prenuclear age preeminence.

But the problem, as the future would reveal, was that flexible response was neither particularly flexible nor responsive. To General Taylor's credit, as Mark E. Swenson points out in the article, "The US Involvement in Vietnam—How and Why" (*page 32, June 1969* AIR FORCE/SPACE DIGEST), the old soldier has admitted as much. He is among the few who have had the grace and intellectual honesty to do so.

Worst still, what conceivably might have worked in Europe —if NATO allies had been willing to beef up their conventional forces to ensure the numerical balance between Warsaw Pact and Western forces claimed by the new men in the Pentagon— had little or no relevance to Asia. But, as Mr. Swenson also points out, flexible response was extended to cover the expected requirements of conflict in Asia and the rest of the so-called underdeveloped world. Counterinsurgency capability (COIN) was added to the flexible response stew. Thus armed, it was believed, we could meet the anticipated challenges of Maoist "wars of national liberation" around the world.

The Administration in power sets the policy tone in Washington, and in John Kennedy's Washington it rapidly became the style to talk of ways and means of countering and conquering borders of sneakered peasants, mesmerized with Maoism, who would soon be assaulting governments, one after another, in Southeast Asia. South Vietnam and Laos were already under siege and Mr. Khrushchev was proclaiming Soviet support of wars of national liberation.

Overnight, there developed a new mystique of counterinsurgency. The Army and Marines were generally enthusiastic. The Air Force, pressed to doff its A-bomb image, reluctantly climbed on the bandwagon. We were all treated to replays of the post-World War II British triumph over the Communist guerrillas in Malaya and we were subjected to endless computations on how many counterinsurgents you needed to cope with and prevail over one Red guerrilla.

But, for a time, it was mostly talk. In Vietnam, the cautious President Kennedy was willing to try out some of the techniques advocated by the counterinsurgency enthusiasts (*again, see*

Mark Swenson's June article for an analysis of the roles of some of the principal Kennedy advisers). But the conflict was then at a low level and the American involvement small. The President had had his fingers burned at the Bay of Pigs, and the Cuban missile crisis had had to be settled by threatening massive retaliation, no less.

What John Kennedy, had he lived, would have done in Vietnam beyond the technical-adviser stage is an "iffy" question that no one, not even Arthur Schlesinger, Jr.—despite his mixed role as adviser and White House note-taker for future memoirs—can really answer. Some argue that, in view of his initial commitment, Kennedy, as disturbed as he was by the repressive Diem regime of the period, would have following the course his successor in the White House took. Others suggest that for a time, during the worst of the Diem days, there was at least a theoretical possibility that Diem's bankrupt regime and its excesses might be used as an excuse for US withdrawal. The weight of evidence favors the first argument, that Kennedy was in Vietnam to stay, if only Diem could be removed in a US-approved coup, which he was.

Both Presidents Kennedy and Diem were removed from the scene by assassination and Vietnam evolved rapidly into a new kind of dilemma. By mid-1964, the US was faced with an even more aggressive North Vietnam, emboldened by what looked like the inevitable collapse of the South Vietnamese regime. And the decisions were in the hands of Lyndon Johnson, advised by the same people, for the most part, who had sold flexible response and COIN to his predecessor. And by now US forces were being restructured to meet the new orthodoxy of flexible response and COIN.

The new President, convinced by the counterinsurgency advocates and by those who put their faith in what they viewed as the cold logic of strategic persuasion that they believed could be applied successfully against North Vietnam, responded with a series of US escalations, which in sum took the US into a full-scale war. The enemy was no longer just the Viet Cong or even North Vietnam but also Red China by proxy. And the newly avowed purpose of US involvement was to prevent the fall of the rest of Asia to communism in keeping with the well-known domino theory.

To say that President Johnson took the country into a major war under circumstances of questionable legality is to belabor the obvious. To ask whether what he did was right or wrong from the standpoint of national interest, in the long run, is to enter a field of argument where no one can tread with certainty. It may well be that the US effort in Vietnam, whatever the final outcome, has sharply altered, perhaps irrevocably, the timetable of Maoist-style revolutions and spurious wars of national liberation and has given non-Communist Asia breathing space to muster the will and force to protect itself and create some decent future for its peoples. We cannot know the final consequences of Vietnam from the geopolitical point of view.

But there is a set of larger, moral, questions that needs to be asked. Did not President Johnson and the coterie of advisers on whom he leaned, including particularly Secretaries McNamara and Rusk, delude themselves and the people by taking the country into a major war stage by stage, almost by stealth, as it were? One having done that, did they not compound the deception by pretending that such a war on such a scale could be mounted without seriously affecting the economy? Was it not a cruel hoax on the poor, who had been promised a war on poverty, to tell them and the country that the war in Asia could be prosecuted without effect on the struggle to overcome domestic problems? The hoax was exposed early when civil rights and anti-war campaigns merged.

And, one may ask, did not the Johnson Administration, particularly the ever-quantifying civilian defense hierarchy, also fail the military who were, after all, the people who had to do the fighting and dying in Vietnam, by running the war as if if it were some species of war game being played out at a think-tank seminar and with small regard for such variables as public opinion and popular support that so often make the difference?

Looked at in this light, the genesis of the Vietnam War become much clearer. We got into this conflict up to our necks, and, it may be added, isolated from virtually all of our allies, as a consequence of military theorizing by a band of planners who in retrospect were largely dilettantes. The irony is that these Strangeloves, for the most part, are now aboard the bandwagon of critics blaming the whole mess on the "military." If the military is guilty of anything, it is a certain impatience with having been given an escalatory game to play with most of the proscriptive rules applied to our side. It is true, and acknowledged above, that there were enthusiasts of limited war and counterinsurgency in all the services. It is doubtless also true that the military, particularly the Army, believed it could win in Vietnam.

But the overriding and immutable fact that the basic policy decisions to go into Vietnam with a force that built up to half a million men were made by the civilian authority. Here the "monolithic" quality attributed by critics to the military *did* obtain: They followed orders. Under our system, should it have been otherwise?

A further irony, of course, is that the North Vietnamese and the Viet Cong turned out to be rather better at the game than our own Strangeloves. For it is *they* who have successfully molded world opinion against America as a bully who bombed the innocent and as the Western busybody who bloodily intervened in a "civil" war.

We have paid an enormous price.

The basic lack of candor about Vietnam, masked primarily by the prestigious public image of Mr. McNamara as the world's greatest manager, lies at the root of almost every major problem the U.S. is currently concerned with. Half of the $80 billion defense budget that the military-industry complex is blamed for is attributable to Vietnam. The desperate fiscal gamble involved in waging the war on a business-as-usual basis, with no restraints on the economy, has fed the flames of inflation. In turn, inflation has eroded the purchasing power of both the government and the private economy.

Defense programs and social programs cost more and hence are more competitive for the tax dollar, exacerbating a conflict in priorities which need not ever have developed. A taxpayers' revolt is brewing. Relations with our allies, particularly in Western Europe, have been strained nearly to the point of rupture at times. The inequities of the draft, especially to feed the needs of a war so open to just criticism, have swelled the ranks of the peace movement, provided a focus for campus dissent, and further complicated the economic and social unrest in the nation.

It is the tragedy of Mr. McNamara and of the country that the impeccable management expert failed to manage his most important assignment. The trappings of efficiency were mistaken for its substance. It is analogous to a hospital being administered with a high degree of competence, except for the fact that patients were dying needlessly. So put the blame on the doctors.

But as important as Vietnam is, as both a symbol and a reality in the search for the real Strangelove, there are other issues that need exploring—ABM, for example.

The chorus of anti-military critics now proclaims that the military and a greedy band of profiteering industrialists are forcing on the country an unneeded and unworkable antimissile system. The critics' argument, depending on who they are, is either that the proposed ABM won't work and is therefore a waste of money, or that, even if it does work, it can't do anything but "force" the Soviet Union to press on with complex offensive weapons that could overwhelm any US defense.

What do the critics offer as an alternative? Nothing less than a total US dependence on offensive weapons sufficient to scare the pants off the Russians and the Red Chinese, plus the hope that the Russians will be gentlemen enough to see the wisdom of meaningful arms-control agreements with us.

The question arises: Who are the Strangeloves here? Under the McNamara Pentagon regime this country accelerated the greatest buildup of offensive power in the history of the world, in keeping with the basic theory of deterrence and in support of the delicate balance of terror. But the problem of virtually total reliance on offensive nuclear power is that if deterrence does not work—let the cause be madness on the part of an enemy or merely a miscalculation— then there *can* be a nuclear war. And if there is a nuclear war, no one can really predict the destruction, no matter how much quantification has been done in advance.

Reason would suggest that if there is a chance, however small, the defenses can be mounted, no rational man would oppose their deployment. Oddly, the most "rational" men of all, the disciples of former Secretary McNamara, those who see him as having brought order to the Pentagon, are among the most vociferous opponents of the idea of bring offensive-defensive balance into US strategic planning. The same people who attacked massive retaliation as devised by John Foster Dulles are now backing that policy, under the label of "assured destruction." Only now the bombs are bigger, and the stakes, if deterrence fails, are even higher than they were in the 1950s.

The ABM issue is thus not so much a question of whether the system the President wants deployed is the best one available—no one can supply the answer to that question barring the test of a nuclear war—but rather whether at long last the United States strategic posture should be allowed to emerge from the Strangelovian shadows of the McNamara era into a new period in which defense can attain some real significance. Despite the claims of those who have written endless numbers of scenarios about assured destruction and all the rest of the jargon of the McNamara era, the world would be *more* hospitable to meaningful arms-control agreements if both the U.S. and Russia developed some measure of strategic defensive capability, by way of having the insurance human beings and governments bank on.

Indeed, rather than calling for U.S. and Soviet pledges *against* deploying defensive systems, serious arms-controllers should be campaigning for an emphasis in arms-control talks on limitations on the *offensive* side. How much more sense it would make in arms talks to *encourage* defensive system development as a preliminary to limiting the deployment of MIRVs and supermegaton bombs!

What the Strangeloves, in their mechanistic approaches to arms control, have not understood, is that arms-control agreements, if they are to have any meaning, must have a base in political reality. And political reality includes the fact that governments, Communist or otherwise, tend to see a duty to afford some measure of defense, if at all technically feasible, for their peoples. Nor do the Strangeloves seems to recognize the quite important arms-control potential in financial terms, of defensive-system development and deployment. For as they themselves suggest, there are limitations to the fiscal resources of even superpowers, as well as continuing resource-allocation problems. Thus, if Russia, the U.S., and other powers began to invest militarily in defensive systems, at least some money otherwise available for offensive developments might not be available.

This possibility never seems to have entered the minds of

such people as Robert McNamara, who in the last analysis is probably the greatest Strangelove of them all, in view of his preoccupation as Defense Secretary with assured destruction and other such abstractions, always on the offensive side.

It is a great irony of our times that Mr. McNamara, who presided over the massive U.S. offensive weapon buildup of the 1960s, is viewed as a kind of hero by so many critics who at the same time claim that "the military" has come to dominate U.S. foreign and domestic policy.

What it all comes down to is that many, many Americans, including a sizable collection of civilians who in recent years have played important executive and advisory roles in the design of U.S. military-political policy, are now angry at the way that power has been deployed by the national leadership. Although many of these people helped write the scenarios, worked the abstract computations, glamorized on paper the beauties of limited war, and peddled the nostrums of counterinsurgency, they now are disowning the stunted children of their musings. The nostrums have not worked and now it is time to find a scapegoat. What more convenient scapegoat than the military? It is so easy to characterize those who have borne the brunt of the battle as having brought about the circumstances that led to the battle. And it is so easy to forget that the conceptual framework of our present policies was built by a corps of "experts," largely outside of the military.

And in these divisive times, scapegoating is a foolish tack. It is silly and dishonest to blame the military per se for the basic mistakes of civilian leaders in the recent past. To do so is just as silly and dishonest as it is to blame the poor for being on the welfare rolls. It makes much more sense to search for the causes of the disasters, in both cases, and to honestly admit the errors of the past so that all of us can learn a little something for the future.

Including the real Strangeloves.

Antimilitarism: Some Hidden Dangers*

Anthony Hartley

Anthony Hartley, formerly with The Economist, *is editor of* Interplay.

Over the last few years, there has been a gradual deterioration of the military image. The favorable portrait of *The Caine Mutiny* has been changed, if not to that of the political generals in *Seven Days in May*, at any rate to something more nearly resembling Norman Mailer's General Cummings in *The Naked and the Dead*. That there are contradictions in the composition does not lessen its impact. To depict an opponent as simultaneously cunning and stupid is the normal small change of polemics.

Nor is the defense establishment likely to benefit much from the fact that many of the charges leveled against it are clearly unfair. As Roger Hilsman [now a Professor in the Columbia University School of International Affairs and author of the recent book *To Move A Nation*] has written, "By 1961 it was a shiboleth among the Joint Chiefs of Staff that the United States ought never again to fight a limited war on the ground in Asia or perhaps never again to fight any kind of war on the ground in Asia."

[United States Marine Gen. David Shoup now retired] seems to believe that their attitude altered after 1964, but it is nonetheless probable that the leaders of the United States armed services were never enthusiasts for intervention on the Asian mainland. This, however, has not prevented them from bearing much of the odium for a political decision which it was their duty to execute as best they could.

Unjust though it may be, a military machine which fights

---

an unpopular war without visibly approaching a successful conclusion will itself become unpopular through the very efforts it has to make to win the undesired conflict. In the same way, while it is clearly the business of professional soldiers to demand (and struggle within the government bureaucracy to get) those weapons which they deem necessary for their task of national defense, this conception of their duties will gain them little thanks from those who wish to earmark the money for other uses.

The controversy over the deployment of an ABM (Safeguard) system has shown clearly enough what gulfs of disbelief statements from the military now have to cross to produce conviction. What has been called the ABM debate has in fact not been a debate at all, but a dual exercise in preaching to the converted. Both sides produced their own scientific experts; neither can be said to have shaken the other by its arguments. What does stand out, however, is that the professional opinion of America's military establishment no longer carries the weight that it once did. Whatever the opinion of the military may have been in the past, they were widely respected as experts in their own field. Now this respect seems to be vanishing. If the Joint Chiefs of Staff cannot compel belief on a subject which most nearly affects the security of the United States, where can they hope to make their influence felt?

Skepticism as to the demands of the armed services is to be welcomed in any country insofar as it forces economy and checks the built-in wastefulness that afflicts all armies and navies. But extreme antimilitarism creates as many problems as it solves. What exactly do some contemporary critics of the military want? Soldiers who do *not* have any influence on policy, who do *not* want the latest weapon systems, who are *not* masters of an efficient fighting machine? Moreover, if the President does not believe his military advisers, whom is he to believe when strategic problems of extraordinary technical complexity have to be discussed? His crystal ball? The academic community (who themselves have conflicting opinions) ?

For it is no good thinking that he can do without military advice altogether. At present the peace of the world depends on a military balance between Russia and the United States which is already being disturbed by developments in technology — multiple independently targeted reentry vehicles (MIRVs), fractional orbital bombardment systems (FOBS), and the like — and may prove very difficult to maintain in future. ABMs are only one element in this complicated situation, whose evolution will depend to a great extent on Russian attitudes and, presumably, on the advice given by Soviet strategists. The 1970s are likely to see any American President facing a number of decisions similar to that resulting in Safeguard — the next one on the list is clearly going to concern MIRV. In approaching them, he might, of course, start from a systematic disbelief in the opinions of his military advisers. But this does not seem likely to be particularly helpful.

At this point in the discussion someone is likely to murmur the words "civilian control." But such control already exists in the United States, perhaps to a greater extent than in most countries (it is, after all, in Russia that a regular soldier is Minister of Defense). Not merely is the American Secretary of Defense a civilian, but the office of Commander in Chief resides in a civilian President as well, and the Department of Defense has to run the gauntlet of congressional committees in order to get the appropriations which it requires. Congressional vigilance can do much to cut down waste and to make sure that hardware costs what the estimates say and not fifty percent more. But the fact must also be faced that, in vital and secret areas of policy such as that of nuclear weapons, there inevitably will be a tendency on the part of any administration to play safe and allow the military at least part of their way. The stakes here are too great to permit the taking of risks, and the avoidance of risks (in the absence of arms-control agreements) implies the development of new weapon systems as the technology for them becomes available.

The permanent threat of long-range nuclear bombardment is bound to force any President to attend to what the Pentagon has to tell him. Military influence on United States policy is built in by the facts of the world situation, being not so much the result of illegitimate pressure as a recognition of the role nuclear strategy now plays in American security. As well as the immediate causes discussed above, the present wave of anti-militarism is also a despairing protest against an international situation which involves the United States in an unending game of nuclear chess as well as in so many commitments around the world.

Behind it lies a generalized dissatisfaction with the course of American foreign policy over the last twenty years.

Under the Kennedy Administration that policy reached its highest point of rationalization, having previously, despite the efforts of intellectuals like George Kennan, consisted of a pragmatic defense of American interests and acquisition of commitments in various parts of the world. From 1961 onward there appears to have been an evolution toward an attempt actually to resolve world problems — in particular, the problem of America's relationship to Russia. For the first time a genuinely global policy was developed (and the fact that it was unsuccessful should not blind anyone to the magnitude of the conception). On the one hand, there was the effort to start a dialogue with Russia; on the other, a determination to cope with "wars of liberation" and "brush fires" in the Third World which might develop into a cause of conflict between the nuclear superpowers. The logic of the Kennedy policy was increased American intervention in local crises — in Vietnam, in the Congo, in the confrontation between Malaysia and Indonesia. The whole construction was the product of intelligent, optimistic rationalists persuaded that something useful could be done by the United States about most foreign-policy problems.

This rationalizing global approach ended in apparent failure in Vietnam, and with its decline has come the decline of those so-called "defense intellectuals" who reasoned so logically about international affairs, but whose sophisticated arguments were so far divorced from the understanding of the general public. Now it is clear that there is a revulsion against the very idea of global power and the burdens imposed by it, and an inarticulate desire to return to an earlier age when only immediate American interests required defense, and the responsibility for settling the affairs of far-off countries lay elsewhere. Of this revulsion, anti-militarism forms part: an attack directed at the most vulnerable sector of America's world policy (it is significant that General Shoup should mention, with some nostalgia, prewar American attitudes as being "typically isolationist, pacifist, and generally antimilitary").

The fundamental questions posed by this attack, whether consciously or unconsciously, are whether the United States needs to maintain the nuclear parity, on which its relations with

Russia rest, and whether it can, or ought to, carry out its obligations to the allies it has acquired in Europe and Asia. The Vietnam War can probably be ended, though disengagement may take longer than is generally thought at the moment, but that will answer only one question about future American commitments. There are many others: Should Thailand receive American military aid? Should Israel be helped in an emergency? How many American troops should remain in Europe?

A rational answer to such questions cannot be found by sudden reductions of United States military strength. Any attempt, in the name of an emotional anti-militarism, to deprive the Administration of the power to make an American presence felt in a given crisis would bring about instability in international relations and perhaps a serious threat to peace. In half a dozen places in the world the United States acts as a stabilizing factor, creating a balance which, if not totally satisfactory, is nevertheless infinitely less explosive than anyone would have dared to hope in 1948. The much-vilified military power of the United States has, in fact, helped bring about conditions in which political negotiations with the Russians may have some chance of success. Its sudden removal or drastic diminution, far from advancing the cause of peace, would reverse the process.

For, so interconnected are the affairs of the world in 1969 that it is no longer safely possible for any country to take purely unilateral decisions (even decisions to withdraw) without regard to the reactions of others. It is perfectly understandable that, at this juncture in their history, the American people should wish to cut back their armed forces and turn to putting their domestic affairs in order. But their ability to do so does not depend upon themselves alone, and any attempt to rid themselves of commitments in defiance of the political balance prevailing in the part of the world concerned will end only in frustration.

In a world where peace still depends upon a balance of power, anti-militarist emotion is as bad a guide to policy as militarist emotion. Diplomacy should be free of both, and devoted to seeking a stable balance where it cannot obtain the abolition of armed force. Ideally (and in a democracy), the armed services should serve the foreign policy of the elected leaders of their country, not create it (it would, for instance, clearly be damaging to American interests as a whole if Okinawa were to continue to be withheld from Japan for technical/military reasons).

But, if this is so, then it follows that it is unjust and unwise to attack the military because they have done their best to execute directives given them by the political leadership. Unjust because they are not responsible for initiating policy. Unwise because too constant and extreme an antimilitarist onslaught risks creating in a professional body of officers bitterness leading in the not so long run to the very type of militarism which the critics fear.

In this instance, as in so many others, extremes create, and feed upon, each other. In terms of civilian-military relations, the worst of all solutions is a powerful military establishment isolated from the country at large and hostile to the civilian government which is its legal master. The present climate of antimilitarism will have done America a disservice if it produces a psychological rift between the society and the armed services which there is some talk at present of completely professionalizing. It will also have done the world a disservice if it creates uncertainty as to the execution of American commitments and ends by leaving a power vacuum in the most crucial areas of international tension.

The Militarization of American Foreign Policy: The Vietnam Experience

Ray C. Hillam

The "increasing militarization of our foreign policy," according to a member of the Senate Foreign Relations Committee, "has been evident in our growing readiness to respond to political problems with military solutions."[1] A prominent American military leader went a step further when he said "militarism in America is in full bloom and promises a future of vigorous self-pollination, unless the blight of Vietnam reveals that militarism is more a poisonous weed than a glamorous blossom."[2] While these views may appear extreme, few would deny the increased role of military elites in the formulation of American policy, particularly in view of the Vietnam experience.

Military advisers yield an immense influence through their role as strategic planners. Unlike their civilian counterparts, they are better organized and more preoccupied with one objective: to meet any threat to the security of the United States through military action. They have their doctrines, discipline and the desire to compete and win. They are technicians, not social scientists. They are "can-do" men, and it is natural for them to say that they can win a war quickly, or that the United States should use military force in the execution of foreign policy in some small country.

1. Senator Eugene J. McCarthy, "The Pursuit of Military Security," *Saturday Review* (December 21, 1968), 8.
2. General David M. Shoup, "The New American Militarism," *The Atlantic Monthly*, 223 (April, 1969), 53.

The Militarization of the Vietnam War

The militarization of American foreign policy has become most evident in Vietnam. While the history of how the United States became involved is long and complicated, yet the crucial decisions which set the course were those decisions which tried to impose a military solution in a country where the problems were mainly political.

When U.S. military advisers took over from the French in 1954, they reorganized the Vietnamese Army into American-type combat formations and trained them to resist an invasion from Vietminh regulars streaming down across the 17th parellel. Thus, they created a roadbound, over-motorized hard-to-supply combat force. In spite of what should have been learned from the French experience with the Vietminh and from the insurgencies in Malaya and the Philippines, the U.S. military advisers attempted to build a modern conventional force, drawing a clear distinction between warfare and politics. Thus, the United States virtually ignored the political problems that were the very basis of the war and relied on a conventional military approach to what was then considered a military problem.

Some years later, with the rise of the Viet Cong guerillas within South Vietnam, President John F. Kennedy and many of his advisers became fascinated with the mystique and virtues of counterinsurgency. Many civilians as well as military leaders pushed the counterinsurgency theme, and by the mid-sixties such actions were partly responsible for taking the United States, stage by stage, into a major through limited war.

Earlier, most civilian and military leaders had deemed it unwise to commit ground forces in Southeast Asia. However, with some changes in the composition of the Joint Chiefs of Staff in 1964 and with the encouragement of each of the services striving to increase their involvement in Vietnam, the United States was hastened into war. The intention at the time was to keep the effort "limited," but as the momentum built up, it became much more than a mere limited or tactical operation. The enemy was no longer just the Viet Cong or even North Vietnam, but also Red China by proxy. And, the newly avowed purpose of U.S. involvement was to prevent the fall of the rest of Southeast Asia to communism.

When military intervention was advised, it is uncertain if the military leaders fully realized the limited character of U.S. objectives. Supposedly, the United States did not intervene to defeat the enemy, but simply to stop the North from taking over the South by force and to permit the people of the South to decide their own future. However, most high level military leaders perceived that the United States was fighting the international communist conspiracy — rather than Vietnamese national communists who did not want to be dominated by either Peking or Moscow.

Soon after the United States became involved militarily in Vietnam, Henry Cabot Lodge arrived in Saigon to commence his second tour as ambassador. He came with the avowed task of promoting a social revolution as an alternative to the Viet Cong movement. He perceived the need to create a large civilian police force to counter terrorism and political subversion, which he presumably felt was more important than to destroy Viet Cong military units on the battlefield.

Consistent with the "counterinsurgency" and "limited warfare" themes of the day, Ambassador Lodge was supposed to be a super ambassador with General William C. Westmoreland responsible for the "military" war and Ambassador William G. Porter in charge of the "other" war. Ambassador Lodge's position was to be strengthened by the presence of an alter ego, retired Major General Edward G. Lansdale, an expert in counterinsurgency. While Porter had the top job in pacification, Lansdale was to be the senior liaison officer to the Vietnamese for pacification.

President Lyndon B. Johnson presumably granted Lodge supreme authority in Vietnam, and on several occasions he tried to strengthen Lodge's position. For instance, he sent one of his White House aides to Saigon with instructions to Lodge, granting him supreme authority over both the military and civilian establishments. At the Honolulu conference in February, 1966, President Johnson took further steps to insure that the military would at all times be subordinated to civilian political judgment in Vietnam. He even sent Vice-President Hubert H. Humphrey to Saigon to dramatize Lodge's desire to sponsor a Vietnamese social revolution as the moral basis of the United States involvement. At the Manila conference in October, 1966, another effort was made to reaffirm the ambassador's role. These measures, however, never really succeeded in stopping the erosion of civilian authority in Saigon.

Ambassador Lodge was either unable to win over the military establishment to his own politically oriented view of what needed to be done or he yielded to their military arguments. Also, while Lodge was given a greater mandate by the White House, he and his civilian subordinates never had the command advantages of military leaders. For instance, Westmoreland could say, "do this, do that," and something would happen. When Lodge would say, "do this, do that," sometimes something happened and sometimes it did not happen. The military, being better organized than the civilians and led by skilled and energetic officers, became dominant. Moreover, the sheer weight of men, money and materials made the military effort more visible and its "progress," measured by the use of body counts, enemy infiltration rates, and air sorties in the North, more dramatic. On the other hand, Ambassador Porter's "other war" was less histrionic and the results less obvious. Thus, Porter's role became secondary and Lansdale became "little more than an idea man, writing long position papers of obscure destination."[3] Clearest evidence of the erosion of civilian influences in Saigon came in the spring of 1967 when the U.S. military took over, in the name of efficiency, the civilian pacification program. Therefore, while Westmoreland was supposed to be subordinate to the ambassador, he assumed, perhaps by default and with reluctance, the role of supreme military commander. And, while Lodge was to be a super ambassador, he became a conventional ambassador. The prominent position of the military in Vietnam continues to this day.

An American Conventional War

Under U.S. military leadership, the Vietnam war became primarily an American conventional war with most of the emphasis on fighting Viet Cong main force units and the North Vietnamese — the kind of war Westmoreland and those around him had fought before and knew how to fight. They felt their duty was to crush the enemy and make him sue for peace. This, they assumed, could be accomplished with more men, more guns, more planes, and more ships; an assumption which led to an almost psychopathic overdependence on firepower. The B-52 raids and the decision to take a battleship out of mothballs and send it to Vietnam are examples of a U.S. conventional military response to the enemy.

By the end of 1967, the war seemed to be moving toward one of "attrition" with the strategy of "grinding down the enemy" until he is forced to give up. But, after months of "grinding," the political infrastructure of the Viet Cong and the Central Office of South Vietnam (COSVN) continued to survive, suggesting that the strategy at best had pruned some branches off the heartwood of the tree.

During the January, 1968, Tet offensive, Westmoreland was correct when he said the "attacks on Saigon" were "of no mili-

---

3. Richard Critchfield, "Our Policies in Vietnam," *The Evening Star* (Washington, D.C.), 9 April 1967.

tary significance," as the enemy sought a political and not a military victory. But, the logic, for instance, of destroying the city of Hue to save it made little sense. The Vietnam war has never been a war for cities or land; some land has been fought over and "won" a dozen times. Moreover, the number and sizes of engagements, the body counts and the discovery of cashed weapons and rice, has had limited meaning in a war which remains essentially political.

For years, the Pentagon had added up the forces on both sides and had predicted what it would take to "win." Yet, the crucial factors have been the loyalties of the peasants, the state of South Vietnam politics, the will of the Viet Cong, and the intentions of Hanoi.

After having committed more than half a million men in a war which cost 25 billion a year, it was argued that because of American national policy of not expanding the war, a military victory in a classic sense was impossible. Today, few military leaders display any enthusiasm for rescue operations involving governments without a popular base or for leadership unwilling to take the necessary steps to save itself. As one former member of Westmoreland's staff said, "Militarily, I wouldn't want to touch a country like Vietnam again with a 10-foot pole."[4]

Washington has always insisted it was South Vietnam's war, yet earlier the South Vietnamese had been removed from the fighting and placed in support of pacification. While it was critical that Vietnamese forces rather than American be placed in support of pacification, it was not necessary to withdraw all of the Vietnamese forces from the battlefield. At the time, senior Vietnamese officers, seeing more and more of their units being sent into secondary roles in the countryside began to speak of the war being an American war. As one Vietnamese officer put it, "for every American soldier you put in this country, it is like telling a South Vietnamese soldier: 'We'll handle this. Don't intrude. We prefer to handle this ourselves.' "[5]

---

4. John T. Wheeler, "Vietnam: Pentagon Says Never Again," *The Salt Lake Tribune*, 7 December 1969.

5. William R. Frye, "Asians Complain U.S. Won't Use Their Troops," *The Evening Star*, 4 October 1967.

Toward "Vietnamization"

Since 1969, the Americanization trend has been reversed. In accordance with President Nixon's Guam doctrine and the policy of Vietnamization, the Vietnamese are returning to the battlefield and the American combat forces are being withdrawn. Unfortunately, because the upgrading of Vietnamese forces was of such low priority during the Americanization of the war, today they are not as prepared as they could be. For instance, at one time it is estimated Westmoreland devoted only 10 percent of his energy to the direction of the Vietnamese forces and 90 percent for the American forces.[6] Nevertheless, the Vietnamese armed services received considerably more attention than civilian security forces such as the police.

While it is important for the Vietnamese Armed Forces to be strengthened, there is a need for a demilitarization of the Vietnamese government bureaucracy and society. While South Vietnam has a "civilian" government, many top positions in Saigon and virtually all in the provinces and districts are still filled by military personnel. The Vietnamese military, instead of the Ministry of Interior or the National Institute of Administration, is training village and hamlet officials at their Vung Thau training center. The Vietnamese National Military Academy, fashioned after West Point, is perhaps the finest educational institution in Vietnam, and the Vietnamese Armed Forces' Political Warfare College is training Political Warfare Officers and assigning them to "political roles" within the armed services.

The U.S. military is well on the road to creating an efficient Vietnamese military establishment such as it did in Korea. But, if the Vietnamese military establishment does not have a sound political and economic base, it will be almost entirely, and perhaps indefinitely, dependent upon the United States. Vietnamization should not only mean the replacement of the American military establishment in Vietnam by Vietnamese, but also the development of a viable political system. If the current trend continues, the American legacy in Vietnam will be more military than a much needed social revolution.

---

6. Wheeler, *op. cit.*

In 1961, President Dwight D. Eisenhower warned that the military establishment and the industry which armed it may some day control American national life. When President Kennedy took office the very same year, the establishment of greater civilian control over the military became an avowed aim. However, when his Defense Secretary, Robert McNamara, left office several years later, the military had even greater influence over American policy than at any time in American history. The challenge and nature of the war in Vietnam was a principal cause for this increasing military influence. It gave impetus to the "military-industrial" complex with its "nucleus of over 410,000 aggressive, ambitious professional military leaders"[7] who at last found an arena in which to apply their skills. It is the Vietnam war which has given these men "their promotions, renown, and sense of being usefully alive."[8] Also, many civilians within the complex have become an intrinsic part of the military apparatus, equally attuned to its viewpoint. And, just as the political nature of the Vietnam war supposedly "civilianized" the thinking of many military elite, so did the thinking of many civilians become "militarized," leading them to seek answers to political problems in conventional military strategy and hardware. It was the civilian adviser, after all, who frequently wrote the scenarios for the Vietnam war, computerized its operations, and glamorized the beatitudes of counterinsurgency and limited war.

Too often, civilians have surrendered to the military responsibility for making broad policy choices and for defining the threats, and the responses to these threats. Thus, they have far exceeded their traditional task of planning battles and training men to carry them out. This loss of balance in the exercise of national choices has produced the dangerously distorted situation in which we find ourselves today.

The recent Cambodian intrusion, in the name of "Vietnamization," once again demonstrates this lack of balance. While the intrusions may be sound policy, the military leaders and President Richard M. Nixon did not take into consideration fully the overall political implications. The U.S. military leaders, it appears, pulled an end run around the State Department in their effort to obtain approval for attacks against the border areas. Secretary of State, William P. Rogers, for instance, was taken by surprise, and Secretary Melvin R. Laird was brought into the planning only in the final stages. Traditionally, a president makes such a decision only after first assuring himself of the support, or at least the consent, of the leadership of Congress, the leaders of his own party, and of the foreign policy experts in the State Department. But, in this case, the President consulted none of these and instead gave his military commanders free rein to embark on the Cambodian campaign in cavalier disregard of the political consequences. It was not, in the American political tradition, a decision made after using the full machinery for consultation. In view of this practice, it is little wonder that the Congressional movement to curb the warpower of the President and his military advisers has received increased impetus.

Conflict and Crisis for National Security*

Charles A. McClelland

Charles A. McClelland is a member of the Department of International Relations, University of Southern California.

I expect that we face an extremely harsh future. The remaining thirty years of this century promise severe stresses and strains for the nation in political, social, economic, and ecological matters. National security is going to be something we shall need to redefine and also something that will have to be fought for with intelligence and determination—with a pursuit as intense as the fight for the ball on the soccer field or the basketball court. The combination of circumstances now unfolding might have been foreseen and prepared for, beginning a generation ago but, instead, the country is not ready and not

* Charles A. McClelland, "Conflict and Crisis for National Security." Remarks prepared for Conference, Annapolis, Maryland, April 6-8, 1970.

yet fully aware of what is coming. We cannot buy back the lost time. It is now obvious that for every dollar spent since World War II to advance nuclear weapon development, we should have spent a matching dollar for the analysis and diagnosis of the dangers and pathologies lurking in the highly modernized, advanced, industrialized, urban society. Of course, we did not even consider doing that. When, with visible self-confidence, we addressed ourselves to the problems of modernization in underdeveloped societies, we should also have been worrying about the precarious conditions of strong but highly vulnerable societies such as our own.

The country as a whole will have to face its trials as they come and will have to learn, as always, from the punishing lessons of history. One can take a comforting, optimistic view that somehow we will prevail and muddle through, if only we keep the faith in the country and its values. That will not be enough in my view: there are far too many ways now fully available for a large, complex, and interdependent society to commit suicide unwittingly. I do not think it wise to put much trust in old solutions. Instead, what might still be done in time is to mobilize a cybernetic device—a steering capability—to guide ourselves away from the edge of a precipice when we approach it too closely. We must, in brief, create somewhere in the society a competent, dedicated, skilled, and well-informed anti-disaster force trained to dissolve situations and disturbances that have become suicidal in character. Two terms sum up for me the cybernetic function for emergency situations: conflict management and crisis control. National security encompasses more than the ability to apply organized force abroad and to suppress violence and civil disorders at home. These are the crude and drastic measures of management and control brought properly into play only when other means and resources have failed decisively. When the term, "the armed services" or the "military establishment" is used, the image of crude and drastic functions employed in desperate, last ditch situations is conjured up instead of an image of skillful and intelligent steering through troubled and difficult situations.

Nowhere in the highly modernized society except in the location now occupied by the armed services can a place be found to build a sufficient standby cybernetic ability to assist society through the more acute phases of major conflicts and crises. We require for the future the development of national security services and not merely armed services; we need an organized concentration of special skills, talents, and information centered on conflict management and crisis control. The evolution in the military establishment begun a quarter of a century ago in this direction should not be halted now as we face rising societal storms but, instead should be advanced into a further stage of development. . . .

An anti-military sentiment has arisen in the country. The armed services already have a somewhat tarnished image; when the post mortem on the Vietnam conflict is ended, it could be still worse. The Secretary of the Navy is worrying in public about the problem of recruiting manpower of high enough caliber to man the technical equipment and facilities of the Navy. Obviously, new and more attractive educational and training programs will need to be instituted, but, in addition, some new concept of service that would advance the welfare of the country should be found. The idea of national service, in circulation for a decade, might be the means to reverse the negative image if it were put into practice. Given the likely post-Vietnam mood in the nation, it is unlikely that any points will be won in overseas activities, however necessary they might be. The military establishment needs to begin adaptive action now; it needs to find ways to participate in national service programs that will build trust and admiration in the public and that will attract young men to join the work.

The foregoing remarks probably are controversial. I should like to make an anticipatory response to my critics and to answer two questions before they are asked: (1) what basis in fact is there for such an alarmist, catastrophic view of the next few decades? and (2) why would I be a willing advocate of a movement that would be, in substance, the creation of a garrison state run by the military who would, if they became as skilled and active as I suggest, exert control over everything in the future society?

There are, I think, two different ways to approach the question of an ominous and trying future. The first is merely to catalog the various social woes now existing and growing and then to project them on the future. Thus, one needs only to run through a long and well-known list of complaints and troubles: the rapid and progressive degradation of the physical and biological environments, the multifarious social and psychological illnesses due to the crowding in cities, the unresolved issues of racial and cultural differences, the threatening instabilities in the economy, the depletion of scarce and essential resources, the rising crime profiles and the loss of efficacy in the judicial systems, the insufficiencies in the social services including the spectacular problems and failures of the educational systems, the manifest shortcomings of the business and industrial communities in meeting social responsibilities, the overloading of city facilities, the withdrawal of trust, particularly among the young in long-standing goals and purposes of the society, the anomie and the growing sense of a lack of community among the populace, the increasing animus abroad against the United States and its foreign policies, the stultification of progress toward international cooperation and the impotency of international organizations to command respect and afford leadership in international enterprises, the unrelieved menace of nuclear war, the serious lag in national political institutions and in political responses to meet the needs in the foregoing situations. Government, it seems, responds in piecemeal fashion only to dramatic episodes arising from one festering situation after another. Government by emergency is, itself, a disaster; what is required is the anticipation of problems before they become crises and the instituting of corrective measures before emergencies arise. The trouble is that all these problems demand concurrent attention. They make up an ecology of their own. Finally, there is the problem of a growing, nagging realization on the part of the better educated, more fortunate, and more sophisticated part of the public (including lately the President of the United States in his State of the Union message) of a progressive loss in the quality of life, both in the public and the private aspects.

All one needs to do after such a recital is to take note of an obvious fact: the chickens are coming home to roost all at once and the time is now and in the next decades. This confluence of severe problems cannot help but generate severe social conflicts because different individuals and different groups will disagree in the midst of confusion on what has to be done, by whom, and by what means. The idea I set forth earlier seems reasonable: the society as a whole and the various elements within it will have to cope as best they can with the problems but we had better plan for and provide resources and organizations capable of guiding inflamed conflicts and their combatants away from final showdowns and senseless violence. It is by no means certain that conflict management can be made to work but we ought to try very hard to make it work.

A second approach to the question is more historical and systemic. This late twentieth century crisis that confronts us is a consequence and later phase of a long development going on over several centuries. In general, it is the modernization process that is behind the troubles. It began in early modern times in western Europe and spread gradually across the globe. It stimulated population growth, science and technology, secular attitudes, urbanization, increasing demands for natural resources, and ever more elaborate social organizations on an increasingly complex, specialized and interdependent scale. It changed fundamentally the ancient life styles of individuals and communities and destroyed the small scale social units within which most men had always lived.

All these intertwined social and technical processes have been evolving at a steadily increasing pace—in effect, the global metabolism has been stepped up constantly although more so in some geographical regions than in others. By the twentieth century, this acceleration effect reached its true takeoff rate. Increasing complexity and a much faster modernization rate became spectacular after World War II. The consequence is described very simply: the numerous social afflictions we noted earlier are system effects of modernization. They are symptoms of dislocations, imbalances, and malfunctions. We are riding in a socio-technical machine that is running out of control and, by failing to have grasped soon enough what is happening, we lack the knowledge and the means to direct it. Our understanding of the complexities of how the machine works has fallen seriously behind the growth of complexity within the machine itself. We do not know how to steer it accurately or how to control its pace. The feeling is that there may be very little time to learn.

The highest priority task is to cope with the lesser collapses, explosions, and upheavals taking place in the machine. This means that acute system breakdowns, or crises, need to be brought under control. The next most important problem, if it can be separated at all from the first, is to keep down panic and frustration among the passengers, especially since the latter blame each other for what is going on and fall readily into fights over the causes and cures of the discomfort being incurred in the rough and dangerous ride. This propensity to fight calls not for the elimination of conflict but instead for its management and buffering when it moves into destructive and escalatory stages. Conflict management should involve more than simple threat and punishment. It would be better to regard conflict management as the application of skilled inducements by a wide variety of means. How to make conflict management effective ought to be one of the chief concerns we have. It is a set of procedures needing both greater development and wider application.

The second question posed above is, in effect, why should we increase and widen the control capabilities of a group—the military establishment—that already unbalances society by its present size, resources, and influence? The direct answer I give is that the most likely way to prevent a garrison state is to replace tendencies toward power, terror, suppression, and coercion with goals and programs which give aid to people in trouble and which help to make repairs to systems—both physical and social—when they have become over-strained or have broken down.

It is argued that military and police organizations attract authoritarian types with a proneness to coerce rather than to reason and persuade and also, individuals with a taste for violence. If this is so, the correction is to change the attracting image and to adjust the organization to prevent domination by such types. In any case, the argument I advanced earlier was in behalf of a transformation away from a strict and narrow military conception of national defense and security and toward an orientation of national security services covering more effectively a wider spectrum of management and control.

As modernized society has become more specialized, fewer and fewer individuals are willing and able to act outside their specialized occupations. More and more people are capable of doing fewer and fewer things for themselves and for others.

They are enchained and immobilized in the division of labor. Long since, the flexible, multipurpose industrial work force gave way to complexes of fixed jobs manned by individuals who could not be assigned to other duties. Contractual arrangements now bind and preserve this system. The same holds in civilian bureaucracies. Only rarely as in the wake of disasters such as floods and earthquakes is there a temporary reappearance of mobile, adaptive, non-specialized work groups. Only in the military services is there a preservation of some of these characteristics on a standing basis. The specific term of service with a pledge to the defense and welfare of the nation, the discipline to guarantee the carrying out of tasks, the power to make reassignments of duty, the responsibility of twenty four hours a day service when necessary, the symbolisms of special status in the uniform and the control over non-duty time and living arrangements, and the strong continuity of organization are a combination of needed attributes not found elsewhere. The absence of one or several of these resources has greatly handicapped the effectiveness of civilian substitute organizations such as the CCC or the Peace Corps. For the purposes of conflict management and crisis control across a wide range of situations, both domestic and foreign and in extremely troubled times there is little choice to be had beyond the armed services. You have to take your pick between an organization that is technically trained but not particularly well-informed and responsive to social situations, and allegedly inclined to coerce to gain control and an organization educated and trained toward responsibility, awareness, and effectiveness in such matters and with a balance of social cybernetic capabilities and technical skills. The second choice is far superior, in my opinion, to the first from almost any angle . . .

The frustration that is really dangerous is that which follows the intervention of armed authority in an acute conflict situation. Forces are called in to quell disorder and are withdrawn as soon as calm is restored. Only an unpleasant coercive action takes place visibly and no opportunity is provided for the restorative, conflict-resolving, remedial acts that should follow. Too often, the situation that became so bad that it produced violence is allowed to lapse back to its previous condition where it smoulders on until the next outbreak. This breeds the frustrations that feed totalitarian movements.

We ought to set up a new national procedure. A social conflict that becomes so bad that it triggers coercive action to abate it ought to be designated for special corrective treatment. Those who intervened should be required to remain, mobilizing all those involved to repair the damage done by the conflict and to correct conditions that led to the trouble. The authority strong enough to quell the disorder should demonstrate that it is also strong enough to solve underlying problems and to set the restorative work in motion. We provide restorative public services, almost automatically, when hurricanes strike and tear up the physical terrain. Why is it that we do not give comparable recognition to social hurricanes that tear up the human terrain? Why is it not the ordinary practice to clean up the debris in the aftermath of a social hurricane and to undertake direct remedial action against a recurrence? To do these kinds of things is what I mean in suggesting the mobilization of talents and resources for crisis management . . .

On the other hand, if the domination of the military industrial complex has gone as far as some of its more vocal critics insist it has, we are dealing with false worries—crying over spilt milk. Presumably, with the capability and the intent to take over the society, it is only a matter of time until the military industrial complex does so. I doubt all this; I have already set forth my view that the real problem is that *nobody* is now equipped to control affairs or to solve our complex and inter-locked set of problems . . .

Chapter Two

The Military Industrial Complex

There has always been a reciprocal relationship between war and technology. Even in societies which relied on the bow and arrow, someone had to make those weapons. In simple societies, of course, warriors frequently made their own weapons, but as societies became more complex weapon making was separated from using them, and each of these functions became specialized roles in society. The interrelationship of armament and technology dictated that each change in technology altered the military balance. Moreover it meant that the traditional values of personal leadership and elan and valor in battle became less important than "fire power" and the network of munition factories on which the fire power rested. It was said in the American West of Judge Colt, the inventor of the Colt 45 revolver, that: "God made men, but Judge Colt made them equal." The implication that the outcome of conflict is determined by superior weapons rather than superior men is a basic lesson of warfare over the centuries. A corollary to that lesson, which makes the search for new weapons so attractive to military planners, is that advances in weapon technology confer upon the innovator a tactical, and, very often, a strategic advantage.

The introduction of new weapons was limited in the past, as at present, by the technological level a society has achieved and by the availability of funds to acquire new weapons. The rate of change of both of these factors until the industrial revolution was relatively slow. During the past two hundred years, however, and particularly in the past hundred years, there has been an accelerating development in man's ability to produce new weapons and his ability to pay for them. This increased ability to create new weapons and to pay for them is a direct result of the industrial revolution. The industrial revolution first of all raised the technological level of society, as it continues to do, beyond what men believed possible in each previous generation, and each change in technology made new weapons possible. One only has to reflect on the changes in warfare wrought by the invention of the internal combustion engine to see that technology ultimately determines military strategy and tactics. The relationship between technology and military tactics is not always clear, but eventually technology is made the servant of warfare; thus, in the period before World War II, the Germans coordinated tanks and airplanes to create a new style of war—**Blitzkrieg.**

The industrial revolution was also responsible for the increased ability of governments to pay for new weapons. Industrial development provides governments with additional sources of taxes: sources which provide far more revenue than taxes on land, for not only can industrial earnings be taxed, but the increased income at all levels of society becomes a fruitful source of taxes. What men want to buy has always been influenced by what they could afford, and certainly the ability to pay for new weapon systems has been a stimulus to acquiring them.

This relationship between the creation of new weapon systems and the ability to pay for them has reached its highest intensity in modern industrial societies—foremost the United States. Moreover, the twin ability to produce weapons and to pay for them, has been achieved almost simultaneously with the development of a deep ideological conflict between the United States and its principal antagonist, the Soviet Union. Stanley Hoffmann has suggested that international relations are most unstable when there occurs simultaneously a change in **what** nations can do to each other and in what they **want** to do to each other. It is precisely this situation which the United States and the Soviet Union have found themselves in since 1945. And it was the general acceptance of the vital necessity to maintain military superiority over the Soviet Union which pushed American weapons development ahead so rapidly in the 1950's and 1960's.

Yet, during most of these years there were stirrings of uneasiness that the goal of maintaining military superiority over the Soviet Union might have unanticipated consequences of momentous importance to the United States. These misgivings were given eloquent expression by former President Eisenhower in his warning about the "military-industrial complex," and that warning has now become the battle-cry of the opponents of the military establishment. President Eisenhower's warning might well have become only a footnote in American history if it had not been for the Vietnamese war, but dissatisfaction with the war and the role of the military in that war has now forced a "great debate" concerning the role of the military-industrial complex in American life. The point at issue seems to be whether the military-industrial complex exists to provide the weapons of war, or whether war exists to provide justification for the military-industrial complex. That debate is the subject of the following selections.

An Evaluation of Its Economic and Social Impact*
The Defense Sector:

Arthur F. Burns

In his famous farewell address, President Eisenhower warned the nation to remain vigilant of what he called "the military-industrial complex." His warning needs to be remembered and pondered by thoughtful citizens. In an age of nuclear weapons, there is no time for assembling the military and industrial forces needed to repel an aggressor. Once a nation is attacked, it can be practically destroyed in a matter of minutes. For this reason as

---

* Arthur F. Burns, "The Defense Sector: An Evaluation of Its Economic and Social Impact," Moskowitz Lecture, New York University, November 1967.

well as because of the unhappy state of our relations with the Communist bloc, "normalcy" for us has come to include since 1950 a formidable military establishment in a state of constant readiness, if need be, for war. But as President Eisenhower observed in his farewell, the "conjunction of an immense military establishment and a large arms industry is new in the American experience. The total influence—economic, political, even spiritual—is felt in every city, who worked, directly or indirectly, on military supplies. Thus the total employment on defense goods and services amounted to $5\frac{3}{4}$ million, or to 86 out of every 1,000 employed workers in the country. Two years later—that is, during the fiscal year which ended this June—the number was nearly $7\frac{1}{2}$ million, or 103 out of every 1,000 employed workers. The employment currently attributable to national security expenditures is even larger; for the figures that I have cited, besides not being fully up to date, take no account of the activities of the Atomic Energy Commission, the National Aeronautics and Space Administration, or other defense-related efforts.

A mere count of numbers, moreover, does not convey adequately the drain of the defense establishment on the nation's work force. Men differ in quality, and we need to take account of the fact that those involved in the defense effort are, on the average, superior from an economic viewpoint to workers engaged in civilian production. Military technology and operations have become very sophisticated in our times. The armed forces now have a highly skilled core and are very selective in accepting men for service. Indeed, the proportion of personnel who completed high school is much larger in the armed forces than in the comparable age group of the civilian population, while the proportion of college graduates is not materially lower. Training and skill count even more heavily among the civilians involved in defense activities. Last year, professional workers accounted for nearly 16 per cent and skilled blue-collar workers for 21 per cent of the civilians employed on defense work, in contrast to about 13 per cent for each of these groups in the rest of the working population. One out of every five of the nation's electrical and mechanical engineers in civilian jobs, two out of every five airplane mechanics, two out of five physicists outside of teaching, and three out of five aeronautical engineers were employed on defense goods during the past year. And even these figures understate the skill dimension of defense employment, for they again leave out of account the highly technical activities originating in the Atomic Energy Commission and NASA.

The heavy emphasis on skill and brainpower in defense employment reflects, of course, the explosion of military technology to which modern science has been contributing so much of its finest energy. Since the Korean War defense contractors have been devoting themselves not only to the production of extremely complex weapons but also to developing entirely new weapons systems that no one as yet knew how to produce. Much of the defense sector of our economy has come to consist, therefore, of research and development work. The President's budget for this fiscal year, for example, allots about 16 billion dollars to research and development, of which 9 billion is to be devoted to defense and another 5 billion to space activities. Since 1960 defense and space programs have consistently accounted for over 80 per cent of the rapidly increasing Federal Funds devoted to research and development. More important still, they have amounted to about 54 per cent of the expenditure on research and development carried out in the entire nation—that is, by the Federal government, industry, universities and colleges, research centers affiliated with universities, and other nonprofit institutions. During the 1950's the proportion of the nation's research and development effort devoted to defense-related activities was only a little lower.

By diverting to its interest so much manpower, especially scientific and engineering skills, the defense establishment has left its mark on both the structure and the functioning of our economy. The effects are all around us. Some defense-oriented industries—notably, the aerospace complex, electronics, and communications—have become a major factor in the economy, and their development has favored many communities—for example, Los Angeles, San Diego, Seattle, and Baltimore. Some large firms have acquired marvelous technological competence from their defense or space contracts and this rather than any immediate profit has commonly been their chief reason for wanting the contracts in the first place. Not a few of the scientists and engineers who received their training in the more sophisticated enterprises have moved into traditional lines of activity, bringing something of the spirit of research and innovation with them. Many of the men released by the armed forces have been able to put the technical skills acquired during their military service to effective use in civilian jobs. And not a few of the processes or products developed for the military have found application in civilian life—for example, jet transports, advanced computers, radar, miniaturized components, and nuclear power plants.

But if the defense sector has stimulated economic development in some directions, it has retarded growth in others. Civilian-oriented laboratories of business firms have often been unable to match the salaries or the equipment that subsidized defense firms offer to scientists and engineers. Research and development work in behalf of new products and processes for the civilian economy has therefore been handicapped. Small firms have derived little benefit from military or space contracts. The draft has added to the labor turnover of all businesses, large and small. The lack of opportunity in the defense sector for poorly educated and unskilled workers has not helped the rural Negroes who have flocked into the cities in recent years in search for jobs and a better life. Moreover, a new class of business executives has arisen, consisting of men whose understanding of marketing and cost controls is often deficient, but who know how to negotiate effectively with government officials handling military or scientific problems. The fact that knowing the right people or having friends in the right places can sometimes advance the interests of a business better than plain business ability has in all likelihood also influenced the management of some firms outside the defense sector.

In any event, the economic growth of a nation is a blind concept unless we consider what is produced as well as the rate of growth of what happens to be produced. During the decade from 1957 to 1966, our nation spent approximately 520 billion dollars on defense and space programs. This sum is about two-and-a-half times as large as the entire amount spent on elementary and secondary education, both public and private. It is almost three times as large as the amount spent on new housing units outside of farms. It exceeds by over a fourth the expenditure on new plant and equipment by the entire business community—manufacturing firms, mining concerns, transportation enterprises, public utilities, and all other businesses. To be sure, an extra billion dollars' worth of bombs or missiles will increase current production just as much as an extra billion of new equipment for making civilian goods. Bombs or missiles, however, add nothing to the nation's capacity to produce, while new equipment serves to augment production in the future. The real cost of the defense sector consists, therefore, not only of the civilian goods and services that are currently foregone on its account; it includes also an element of growth that could have been achieved through larger investment in human or business capital. But even if we assumed that the conflicting influences of the defense sector on economic growth canceled out, its real cost is still enormous.

Unhappily, we live in dangerous times which make large national security expenditures practically unavoidable. Nevertheless, there are always some options in a nation's foreign and military policy, and we therefore must be alert to the opportunities that our military establishment forces us to forego. For example, if the resources devoted to military and space activities during the past decade had been put instead to civilian uses, we could surely have eliminated urban slums, besides adding liberally to private investment in new plant and equipment as well as both public and private investment in human capital.

III

The military-industrial complex, of which President Eisenhower spoke so perceptively in his farewell address, has therefore been affecting profoundly the character of our society as well as the thrust and contours of economic activity. Nor have the social effects been confined to the kinds of goods that we produce. Hopefulness about the future, optimism about success of new undertakings, impatience to complete satisfactorily, whatever is begun—these phychological qualities have been peculiarly American characteristics, and they account in far greater degree than we may realize for the remarkable achievements of our economic system and the vigor of our political democracy. These qualities are deep-rooted in American experience and they continue to sustain us. Nevertheless, the development and spread of thermonuclear weapons, the frustrations of the cold war, and now the brutal struggle in Vietnam have left us, despite our awesome military power, more anxious about our national security than our fathers or grandfathers ever were.

Adults whose habits were formed in an earlier generation

may put the danger of nuclear catastrophe out of mind by losing themselves in their work or by seeking solace in religion. That is more difficult for our children who increasingly wonder what kind of world they have inherited by our doings. There can be little doubt that the lively competition among the great powers in devising instruments of terror is one of the underlying causes of the restlessness of modern youth.

Moreover, young men of military age are bearing a disproportionately large part of the defense burden. That is unavoidable at a time of war, but our generation has institutionalized compulsory military service even when the nation is at peace. It is undoubtedly true that many young men derive deep satisfaction from serving their country as soldiers, sailors, or aviators. Not only that, many have also found useful careers in the armed forces, or have benefited in their civilian jobs from the skills acquired during military service, or have gained a larger understanding of life by associating with men of widely different backgrounds or by being stationed abroad for a time. Despite these benefits, the draft has by and large proved to be a seriously upsetting factor in the lives of young people. Not knowing when they would be called up for military service or whether they would be accepted, many have found themselves marking time. Those who are accepted have often had to interrupt their schooling or careers, perhaps alter plans with regard to marriage, and in any event be content with substantially lower pay than they could earn as a rule in civilian work. Moreover, the administration of the draft over the years, particularly the handling of student deferments, has raised troublesome moral questions in the minds of young people—and, for that matter, in the minds of older citizens as well. . . .

The highly specialized aerospace, electronics, and communications industries will probably not bear much of the burden of post-Vietnam cutbacks. On the contrary, once the curve of military spending turns upward again, as it well may two or three years after the ceasefire, these are the very industries that are likely to benefit most from the dynamism of modern technology. To maintain a sufficient strategic superiority to deter any agressor, we have been devoting vast sums to research and development, as I have already noted. The fantastic new weapons and weapons systems devised by our scientists and engineers soon render obsolete some of the existing devices, which themselves were new and revolutionary on a short time ago. But while the new devices are being built, those that were only recently new cannot yet be abandoned and may even need to be augmented. Costs, therefore, tend to multiply all around. Meanwhile, the Soviet Union has been striving through a remarkably enterprising and inventive military-industrial complex of its own to establish military parity, if not actual supremacy. For example, we have recently learned of the deployment of an anti-ballistic missile system around Moscow and Leningrad, of a novel ship-to-ship missile of Russian origin fired in the Mediterranean, and of the apparent development of an orbital bomb capability by the Soviet Union. Communist China has also been developing, and with greater speed than was generally anticipated, the ability to make and deliver sophisticated weapons. In turn, our military establishment, besides innovating vigorously on its own, keeps devising countermeasures to what the Russians or Chinese have or may have in hand. Both its reaction and its fresh challenge to potential aggressors can be expected to become stronger once Vietnam no longer requires top priority.

As we look beyond the cessation of hostilities in Vietnam, we therefore need to recognize that the scale of defense expenditures has, in effect, become a self-reinforcing process. Its momentum derives not only from the energy of military planners, contractors, scientists, and engineers. To some degree it is abetted also by the practical interests and abilities of ordinary citizens. Any announcement that a particular defense installation will be shut down, or that a particular defense contract will be phased out, naturally causes some concern among men and women who, however much they abhor war and its trappings, have become dependent for their livelihood on the activity whose continuance is threatened. With a large part of our economy devoted to defense activities, the military-industrial complex has thus acquired a constituency including factory workers, clerks, secretaries, even grocers and barbers. Local chambers of commerce, politicians, and trade union leaders, while mindful of the interests of their communities, may find it difficult to plead for the extension of activities that no longer serve a military purpose. Many, nevertheless, manage to overcome such scruples. Indeed, candidates for the Congress have been known to claim that they are uniquely qualified to ward off military closings or even to bring new contracts to their districts, and their oratory has not gone unrewarded by the electorate. The vested interest that many communities have in defense activities is thus likely to continue to run up costs on top of the rising budgets generated by the momentum of competing military technologies. Not only that, it will continue to suggest to many foreign citizens, as it sometimes does even to our own, that our national prosperity is based on huge military spending, when in fact we would be much more prosperous without it.

If the picture I have drawn is at all realistic, the military-industrial complex will remain a formidable factor in our economic and social life in the calculable future. It will continue to command a large, possibly even an increasing, part of our resources. It will continue to strain Federal finances. It will continue to test the vigor of our economy and the vitality of our democratic institutions. For all these reasons it will also generate political tensions in our society, as the widening and bitter debate over Vietnam plainly indicates.

Two schools of political thought are now locked in a contest for the mind and soul of America. One school looks outward, the other looks inward. One school draws much of its strength from the revolution of military technology, the other from the revolution of rising expectations. One school sees communism as a centrally directed conspiracy against the Free World, the other sees it breaking up into independent national movements. One school sees our survival as a free people threatened by communism, the other sees the main threat to free institutions in the deterioration of our cities and the sickness of our society. One school seeks overwhelming military power to deter fresh communist adventures, and is willing to risk war in order to prevent the geographic expansion of communism.

The other school seeks wider social justice and better economic conditions for Negroes and others who have not participated fully in the advance of prosperity, and holds that the force of moral example can contribute more to our national security than additional bombs or missiles.

Both schools have focused their attention on the Federal budget and neither has been satisfied by the treatment accorded its claims. From 1955 to 1965, Federal spending on non-defense activities increased faster than on defense. Since then, defense expenditures have gone up more rapidly, though not much more rapidly. Looking to the future, professional economists frequently point out that our growing economy will make it possible to have more butter and also more guns, if they are needed, even as we have been managing to do while the war in Vietnam is being waged. Their reassurance, however, does not satisfy those who feel that our national security requires not just more guns, but many more guns. Nor does it satisfy those who feel that we need much more butter and that our statistics of the gross national product are misleading us by their failure to allow for the pollution of our water, the poisons in our air, the noise of our streets, the roaches and rats in our slums, the rioting in our cities, or the destruction of life on our highways. Debate along these lines has reached a high point of intensity as the war in Vietnam has dragged out. It has become a divisive force, and it has brought anguish to our people. Its effect on the conduct of the war, however, is likely to count for less than its effect on the general direction of our foreign and military policy in the future.

For the debate is demonstrating to thoughtful citizens that our national security depends not only on awesome military forces, but also on the strength of our economic system and the wholesomeness of our social and political life. As this lesson sinks in, we will want to try far harder than we ever have, both in our personal capacity and through our government, to bring the mad armaments race under decent control. And if the cracks of freedom within the communist system of tyranny widen, as they well may in coming decades, we can be sure to be joined in this quest by the people of the Soviet Union and eventually by the people of mainland China as well. That, at any rate, is the only hope for saving ourselves and the entire human family from catastrophe.

Growing Threat of Our Military-Industrial Complex*

Jack Raymond

Jack Raymond is the author of *Power at the Pentagon,* published in 1964. For many years he was a correspondent for the *New York Times,* writing from Europe after World War II until returning to the United States in 1956 to cover defense affairs from Washington for almost ten years. Formerly Vice President of Clifton-Raymond Associates, he is now President of the Thomas J. Deegan Company, Inc., public relations consultants in New York.

Several months before he was due to leave office, President Dwight D. Eisenhower asked Dr. Malcolm Moos, his special assistant and speech writer (now President of the University of Minnesota), to put together some material that could be used in a farewell address to the nation. Eisenhower, who has a sense of history that too often has been overlooked by his detractors (with the exception of one writer, who speculated that the old soldier thought of himself as George Washington and therefore also wanted to be remembered for his farewell speech), told his assistant that he wanted something more than a platitudious onward-and-upward Presidential sermon.

Dr. Moos, as was his custom for many major speeches, gathered excerpts of Eisenhower memoranda and some jottings based on extemporaneous remarks the President had made to small groups at the White House, and he added a few ideas of his own for the President's consideration. In their second or third discussion of the planned valedictory, Eisenhower suggested, "Let's bring Milton in, and we can meet regularly to put this in shape." Thereupon the President's brother, Dr. Milton Eisenhower, joined in a series of lengthy late-evening sessions at the White House that resulted in the now-famous parting

---

* Jack Raymond, "Growing Threat of Our Military-Industrial Complex," *Harvard Business Review* (May-June 1968).

warning against the dangers of the "military-industrial complex."

Whether or not he thought of matching Washington, President Eisenhower's farewell address, on January 17, 1961, may well be quoted long after the First President's parting admonition against permanent alliances with foreign nations. For while foreign alliances have become an accepted form of America's projection of power in modern times, a society based on war and the threat of war is so alien to the American self-image that even today, in time of war, the ingredients of military preparedness evoke stereotyped suspicions of unseen provocateurs and profiteers. . . .

Arms Industry Under Fire

In his farewell address, Eisenhower reminded the American people that the United States, which until World War II had not had an armaments industry, was no longer able to risk emergency improvisations of national defense. It has been "compelled to create a permanent armaments industry of vast proportions" in support of a huge defense establishment costing more than the total net income of U.S. corporations. He pointed out:

"This conjunction of an immense military establishment and a large arms industry is now in the American experience. The total influence—economic, political, even spiritual—is felt in every city, every state house, every office of the Federal government. We recognize the imperative need for this development. Yet we must not fail to comprehend its grave implications. Our toil, resources and livelihood are involved; so is the very structure of our society.

"In the councils of government, we must guard against the acquisition of unwarranted influence, whether sought or unsought, by the military-industrial complex. The potential for the disastrous rise of misplaced power exists and will persist.

"We must never let the weight of this combination endanger our liberties or democratic processes. We should take nothing for granted." The foregoing is the passage that is most often quoted, but Eisenhower went on to sound the warning of a subtler, and perhaps more fundamental, alteration in the American system:

"Akin to, and largely responsible for the sweeping changes in our industrial-military posture, has been the technological revolution during recent decades.

"In this revolution, research has become central; it also becomes more formalized, complex, and costly. A steadily increasing share is conducted for, by, or at the direction of the Federal government.

"Today the solitary inventor, tinkering in his shop, has been overshadowed by task forces of scientists in laboratories and testing fields. In the same fashion, the free university, historically the fountainhead of free ideas and scientific discovery, has experienced a revolution in the conduct of research. Partly because of the huge costs involved, a government contract becomes virtually a substitute for intellectual curiosity. For every old blackboard there are now hundreds of electronic computers.

"The prospect of domination of the nation's scholars by Federal employment, project allocations, and the power of money is ever present—and is gravely to be regarded."

Venerable Prejudices

There, then, is the Eisenhower warning. Many found it surprising that a military man whose best friends were big businessmen should have uttered it. But it was consistent with his frequently expressed concern over the pressures that had assailed him in the White House. It was consistent also with the historical heritage of the country. For fear of, and aversion to, military influence are rooted deep in the American psyche. The English quartering of a standing army on colonial soil to fight the French and Indian Wars was one of the causes of the American revolution. The writers of the Declaration of Independence complained that King George had "affected to render the military independent of and superior to the Civil Power."

Moreover, there was cause enough in the American experience to question the motives behind defense buildups and arms purchases. Two American authors, H. C. Engelbrecht and F. C. Hanighen, contributed a lasting phrase with the title of their book, *Merchants of Death*.[1] The book reports on a Congressional investigation in 1929 which disclosed that an "observer" for U.S. shipbuilders had tried to wreck the 1927 Geneva Naval Reductions Conference. The case came to light when the "observer" sued the shipbuilders for fees he claimed were due him for his work. It brought a public protest from President Herbert Hoover.

A Senate investigation conducted by Gerald P. Nye in the 1930's concentrated on the great profits made by defense manufacturers in World War I; it did much to arouse American suspicions that the arms makers were responsible for wars. President Franklin D. Roosevelt, pledging his cooperation with the Nye investigation, attributed the "mad race in armaments ... in no small measure to the uncontrolled activities of the manufacturers and merchants of engines of destruction." Even in World War II there were many who blamed the "creeping involvement" of the U. S. economy in the war for America's ultimate participation in it.

Insidious Influence

Eisenhower's concern over the "complex" was based to a considerable extent on military spending pressures on his budget. At the height of a particularly aggravating dispute over the respective merits of Army and Air Force antiaircraft weapons, he declared that "obviously political and financial considerations" rather than "strict military needs" were influencing the weapons debate. And on another occasion, when asked whether he would be willing to allocate more money for defense if the nation could, as his critics insisted, afford it, he replied heatedly. "I would not." Anyone "with any sense," he said, knew that if military spending were not restrained, the country would become a "garrison state."

Reflecting afterward on his experiences, Eisenhower confirmed his "uneasiness about the effect on the nation of tremendous peacetime military expenditures." He complained in his memoirs. "The military services, traditionally concerned with 100 percent security, are rarely satisfied with the amounts allocated to them, out of an even generous budget."[2] As for private industries, they were spurred by the desire for profits and created "powerful lobbies to argue for even larger munitions expenditures." Regarding political influence, he added, "Each community in which a manufacturing plant or a military installation is located profits from the money spent and jobs created in the area."[3]

The war in Vietnam has also raised understandable questions as to the country's vested economic interests. In the last two years alone the intensification of the war in Vietnam has created more than a million jobs in the United States. The sharp rise in employment amounted to 23% of the total increase of more than 4 million jobs in the economy during 1966 and 1967. Toward the end of 1967, defense work accounted for 5.2% of the nation's total civilian employment, up 3.9% in two years. The Vietnam buildup since 1965 increased jobs in virtually all industries, including more than 141,000 new jobs in the aerospace industry, 10,000 in the communications equipment industry, 74,000 in transportation, 30,000 in the clothing industry, 30,000 in iron and steel manufacturing, and 12,000 in the food industry.

It is evident, however, that in his farewell address Eisenhower was not warning of some nefarious conspiracy by military and industrial leaders (although he was more alert than most Americans to the political savvy of seemingly nonpolitical military men). He explained at his final news conference as President that he was not thinking so much of willful misuses of power as of "an almost insidious penetration of our own minds that the only thing the country is engaged in is weaponry and missiles and—I'll tell you we just can't afford that."

Complex Anatomy

To understand and assess the military-industrial complex, we must identify it and consider its magnitude, its composition, and the interaction of its component parts.

The military-industrial complex includes all those elements of American society—economic, political, and professional—that have a material or philosophic stake in a large defense establishment. It includes not only the Armed Services and the companies that produce for them, but politicians in and out of government, workers and union leaders, ordinary citizens and local officials, teachers in schools, and academicians—in short, all who for reasons of "pork or patriotism" support the Armed Forces" requirements.

It may be simplistic to bundle diverse elements of the miltary-industrial complex into a single "it," but "it" is very real, as former Secretary of Defense Robert McNamara attested after seven years in his post. Characteristically, McNamara asserted he rarely lost to "it." He told an interviewer. "I'd say in this area we haven't lost more than 2% of the cases to the so-called military-industrial complex—and in those instances we failed to present our case properly." But what about the magnitude of the cases lost? Even a straight-across-the-board 2% of Pentagon expenditures in the nine budgets McNamara worked on in seven years, including estimates for fiscal year 1969, totals $10.3 billion—twice the estimated cost of the anti-China ABM defense system, which is considered by many to be the "complex's" latest prize.

Our Beneficent Budget

The Pentagon's spending program supports not merely the tactics and strategy of the fighting fronts; it reaches into the lives of all of us on the domestic front. Allocations for military research spin off into jobs and products that can and do become important to the civilian economy. The decision to open a base or close one can affect grocery store owners and church fathers as well as night club operators and liquor dealers. The confluence of interests in the military budget thus results in unusual alliances as varying segments of society, motivated by momentary or social objectives, seek each other's support for shares of Pentagon expenditures . . .

Numerous Beneficiaries

There are various ways of looking at Pentagon spending. To begin in quantitative terms, consider the spread of contracts:

Some 22,000 prime contractors and 100,000 subcontractors enjoy the defense business that is generated in different military programs.

A total of 76 industries, from aircraft to X-ray apparatus, are classed as defense-oriented.

Plane makers and shipbuilders derive more than half their income from defense contracts.

About 5,300 U.S. cities and towns boast at least one defense plant or company doing business with the Armed Forces.

The Armed Forces have swelled to more than 3,490,000, a jump of about 800,000 in two years. The number of persons employed directly or indirectly because of military spending has risen to 4,100,000 men and women—about 1,000,000 more than last year. The number of Americans in the uniformed services and in defense-generated employment of all kinds is said to account for nearly 10% of the entire U.S. labor force of 78,000,000.

Then there are the Pentagon's direct economic holdings. The Pentagon is landlord over some 27.6 million acres of land in the United States; this land is valued officially at $38.4 billion—and some of the values have been calculated in terms of prices of more than a century ago! The Military Services and Defense Agencies, after a calculated effort to rid themselves of costly installations, still maintain some 470 major bases, camps, and installations and about 5,000 lesser ones around the nation. The Department of Defense budget for nine arsenals in the current fiscal year totals $3.9 billion, up $2.6 billion from last year. These arsenals employ 57,000 workers and are operating at full capacity because of the war in Vietnam.

Big Contractors

Another way of looking at the defense contracting business is to examine the military prime contract awards of $10,000 or more which the Pentagon regularly lists by state, region, and commodity categories. In fiscal year 1967, the most recent period for which figures have been made available, 100 companies accounted for 65.5% of the military prime contracts.

The top military contractor for that year was the McDonnell-Douglas Corporation, which represented the merger of two companies that had been among the country's leaders. This company received over $2.1 billion in defense contracts, accounting for 5.4% of the total awarded. McDonnell-Douglas produces the F-4 Phantom series of fighters and reconnaissance aircraft. The General Dynamics Corporation, with over $1.8 billion in defense contracts, accounting for 4.7% of the total, was second on the list. General Dynamics, whose contracts include the F-111 (TFX) aircraft, as previously mentioned, also produces missiles and ships. Lockheed Aircraft Corporation was the third largest contractor in fiscal 1967, with $1.8 billion; General Electric Company was fourth, with more than $1.2 billion; and United Aircraft Corporation was fifth, with nearly $1.1 billion. The top ten included the American Telephone and Telegraph Company, in eighth place with $673 million in defense contracts.

Some states are well favored by the largest contractors and therefore posses stronger interests than others in the perpetuation of the system. California was at the top of the list, with over $6.6 billion, which comprised 17.9% of the total. The identity of the second state on the list led one reporter to write:

"President Johnson's home state of Texas, which only a few years ago ranked seventh among the states getting prime defense contracts, now has nosed out New York for No. 2 spot, Pentagon figures showed today."[4]

Although there are many changes from year to year in the list of prime contractors, the cluster at the top is a "hard core." Eight of the top ten prime contractors in fiscal 1967 were in the top ten in the period 1958–1960; seven, in the period 1951–1953; and six, in the period 1940–1944. Four companies—Douglas (now part of McDonnell-Douglas), Lockheed Aircraft, General Electric, and United Aircraft—have been in the top ten for the past 23 years.

Marietta on the Make

The benefactions of defense contracting appear more dramatic still when specific examples are considered. One good illustration is the city of Marietta, Georgia. Lockheed-Georgia Company, a division of Lockheed Aircraft Corporation, is located in Marietta and is the largest single industrial organization in the Southeast. About 90% of Lockheed-Georgia's business stems from defense contracts, the most important of which now are for the development and building of the C-5A military transport (worth about $1.4 billion) and the production of the C-141 Starlifter (worth another $600 million or more).

Lockheed-Georgia pays about $200 million a year in wages to 26,000 workers drawn from about 55 of Georgia's 159 counties— about one third of the state. Marietta's mayor, Howard Atherton, has said the impact of Lockheed-Georgia on his city's economy is "almost immeasurable." Robert Cox, a Machinists Union leader in Marietta, said defense spending "would almost have to be considered a major ingredient in the continuing low rate of unemployment in the metropolitan Atlanta area." Lockheed buys everything from soft drinks to metal parts from Georgia suppliers. Last year, the company spent $113 million with about 1,720 suppliers, many of them small businesses . . .

Arms for Sale

No review of U.S. defense business would be complete without inclusion of the government's own mercantile interest in it, for the United States engages in the sale of arms as a source of revenue for the Treasury. In fact, the United States is the world's principal arms supplier. This is not surprising, or novel. The United States was the arsenal of democracy in two world wars. And in the period immediately after World War II, it maintained its role as arms supplier in order to bolster Western Europe against threatened Communist aggression.

From 1949 to 1962 the U.S. Government alone (not counting private arms sales) sold $16.1 billion worth of military arms to other countries and gave away about $30.2 billion. Since 1962, when the current arms sales program began, Pentagon officials have been as aggressive as private arms merchants, with the result that the United States has sold over $11.1 billion worth of arms. In a speech in Los Angeles in the spring of 1966, the Pentagon official in charge of the sales program proudly estimated that it had yielded $1 billion in profits for American industry and 1.2 million man-years of employment for companies throughout the country.

So aggressive has been the Pentagon in selling abroad that for several years it managed to use the Export-Import Bank to provide easy credit for poorer, underdeveloped nations, much like the easy-credit terms that flourish between retailers and ghetto inhabitants.

Congress, angered by disclosures of socalled "Country X" accounts, ended the practice in 1967 and put ceilings on the grants and sales of arms to Latin America and Africa. However, the sale of arms abroad continues to be a big—very big—business.

Wooing of the TFX

The TFX story is probably the most outstanding example of the pressures that can be identified in the military-industrial complex—pressures that are still reverberating, in this case, more than five years after the initial Pentagon announcement of the award of a potential $7 billion contract to the General Dynamics Corporation.

The TFX (Tactical Fighter, Experimental), later named the F-III, a jet fighter-bomber, was the biggest contracting plum since World War II. The competition for the contract developed between Boeing, with headquarters in Seattle, and General Dynamics, with corporate headquarters in New York. Boeing planned to place the work in its Wichita, Kansas plant; General Dynamics planned to develop and build the plane in its Convair division at Fort Worth, Texas.

Inevitably, the politics of geography drew public notice. The then Vice President, Lyndon B. Johnson, was from Texas; the first Secretary of the Navy in the Kennedy Administration, John B. Connally, was Governor of Texas and a close friend and associate of Johnson; and the then Secretary of the Navy, Fred Korth, was one of the most prominent citizens of Texas. A Congressional committee brought out the fact that the bank of which Korth had been president held the General Dynamics checking account in Forth Worth.

Meanwhile, a number of members of Congress were also interested in the TFX award:

Several of them were in touch with Secretary of the Air Force Eugene Zuckert during the contract negotiations. One of them, Senator Mike Monroney of Oklahoma, said later he had visited Zuckert's office "to remind him of the vast government-owned plant in Tulsa, Oklahoma, which the Douglas Aircraft Company operates, and its large unused machinery and manpower capabilities."[5]

Senator Stuart Symington of Missouri, a former Secretary of the Air Force, visited Zuckert to discuss the possibility of Missouri companies obtaining subcontracts from whichever manufacturer got the prime contract.

Senator Warren Magnuson of Washington inquired about the status of the competition. His fellow Washingtonian, Senator Henry M. Jackson, frequent butt of the jape that he is the "Senator from Boeing," openly said he had insisted on an investigation when Boeing did not win the contract.

Senators Frank Carlson and James B. Pearson, and Representative Garner E. Shriver, all of Kansas, where Boeing had an idle plant at Wichita, visited Zuckert as a group and told the Air Force Secretary that Boeing could do the job better than its competitor.

Representative Jim Wright of Fort Worth, Texas, made no bones about his interest and the reason for it:

"In the absence of a substantial contract of this type, the General Dynamics team at Fort Worth was faced with dismemberment. It meant the difference between employment or unemployment for thousands of my constituents. Let me be completely frank. I talked about this subject with everybody I could get to listen, both military and civilian officials. That does not in my judgment amount to undesirable political influence. The same sort of thing was being attempted by the other side."[6]

Unnecessary Contracts?

In the case of the TFX there was at least general agreement on the desirability of such an airplane. However, some large weapons programs have been pushed hard by the military-industrial complex when there were contentions that they were not needed at all. The United States has spent almost $19 billion since World War II on missile systems that either were never finished or were out of service when finished because of obsolescence. And the story might have been worse. The B-70 is

an example of a major weapons system that Air Force leaders—
and security-minded supporters, including contractors—persis-
tently advocated; it was rejected successively by the Eisenhower,
Kennedy, and Johnson administrations on the ground that it was
(or soon would be) outmoded. Score that one *against* the power
of the military-industrial complex.

Controversial ABM: Only the future will tell how to score
the $5 billion ABM system which is being designed to protect
the United States against a possible ballistic missile attack by
Communist China in the 1970's.

The Army has been pushing an antimissile defense for more
than ten years and has patiently suffered the scorn of those who
first said that it was impossible and now argue that it is too expensive.

As long ago as 1957, General Maxwell D. Taylor, when he
was Chief of Staff of the Army, appealed for a $3 billion start
on such a system, and he found means of getting his top-secret
proposal into the press after he ran up against opposition in
the Eisenhower Administration. In 1961, with Taylor back in
favor at the White House under Kennedy, the Army renewed
its campaign. *Army,* the magazine published by the Association
of the U.S. Army, featured articles by generals praising the
Nike-Zeus ABM system and advertisements by Western Electric
and eight subcontractors for the project. The issue contained
a map showing 37 states that were already sharing in the research and development work and were likely to get more if
production were approved. Next the House and Senate rang
with speeches calling for Nike-Zeus production to start immediately. And in 1963 Senator Strom Thurmond, a reserve general
in the Army, forced the first secret session of the Senate since
World War II in an effort to win an appropriation for a production start on an American antimissile defense. He lost. The
Kennedy Administration successfully resisted that pressure.

But now, ten years after the start of the campaign, the
Johnson Administration has relented in part. A full ABM defense network against a possible missile attack from the U.S.S.R.
is still considered pointless to undertake—it would cost more
than $30 billion under existing conditions—because the Soviets'
ballistic missile force is so powerful that the ABM defense

admittedly could not cope with it. But for a decade, at least, a so-called "thin" defense against China is said to be worthwhile. Why? Near the end of his term as Secretary of Defense, McNamara tied himself in knots explaining why, the heart of his justification being that a ten-year insurance policy against a relatively small Chinese Communist nuclear missile force was worth $5 billion. Arguments that this might start a new arms race were rejected.

Votes for ABM: Long before McNamara made his announcement, Frederic W. Collins, Washington correspondent for the Ridder newspapers, drew attention in an article in *The New Republic* to some of the ingredients that finally may have broken resistance to the ABM.[7] He noted the favorite ploy of the industrial side of the complex, this time an advertisement in *The New York Times* financial section by the investment firm of Arthur Wiesenberger & Co., which offered a special report on nine companies involved in the research and development of Nike-X (forerunner name of the ABM). The advertisement listed the 28 potential corporate beneficiaries of the Nike-X development program. Collins stimated that the 28 companies had about 300 plants in 42 states plus Puerto Rico and Washington, D.C., and offered a "conservative guess" that they provided jobs for 1,000,000 employees. The writer then noted that the plants were in the domain of 84 Senators and 172 Representatives.

Conclusion

Having identified, described, and examined certain aspects of the military-industrial complex, we must consider its implications for us. Could the United States become a garrison state in which most of its energies are devoted to arms? Could the pressures of war and the frustrations of international affairs pave the way to a military coup such as that depicted in the novel *Seven Days in May?* Are the appeals for peace and disarmament being selfishly balked by the vested interests of the military-industrial complex? These are ancient forebodings in U.S. history, and the fact that they linger reveals a national awareness of our vulnerability. For it cannot be denied that the military-industrial complex flourishes in war and during the threat of war.

Checks and Balances

Yet this awareness of our vulnerability itself constitutes considerable protection for us. For example, we are often troubled by the intervention of the military in "civilian" affairs. But we can take encouragement from the very openness of that intervention. When General Earl G. Wheeler, the Chairman of the Joint Chiefs of Staff, boldly and publicly disagrees with the Secretary of Defense on policies for the war in Vietnam or on the desirability of constructing a full-scale antiballistic missile defense system, and when General Wallace M. Greene, the commandant of the Marine Corps, publicly demands a greater national devotion to the war in Vietnam than to the social revolution in the streets of America—these expressions by the military serve to identify them publicly with recognizable political attitudes. By joining the public debate in a manner that is authorized under our system, they also set themselves up as targets in that debate.

Moreover, as we have learned from experience, the military are not always unanimous in their professional view of the world and in their demands on the budget. Their rivalries for funds have sometimes exploded in fierce public lobbying and internecine bureaucratic warfare. This, too, mitigates against concerted action by the military to influence public policy. In addition, far from challenging civilian control, the military leaders in recent years have complained of civilians dominating the military in their professional competence, The complaint does honor to the principle of our democratic system.

Insofar as the economic threat of the military-industrial complex is concerned, it appears to reflect largely the familiar dangers of huge concentrations of economic power. And there is recurring evidence of the government's capacity to cope with the industrial giants. During the Kennedy Administration we saw the Secretary of Defense lead the charge against a sudden increase in the price of steel. In the Johnson Administration, in November 1965, the Defense Secretary also led in thwarting aluminum and copper price increases by threats to use the national stockpiles.

Another safety factor is that not all states and communities share equally in the defense business despite the fervent Administration activities of the military-industrial complex, even within its own constituencies. The result is high-pitched competition involving defense contractors and their political, military, legislative, and other allies. A single defense appropriations bill usually occupies several dozen members of Congress and several committee staffs for the better part of six months, and not all of these Congressmen have the same concerns and motives.

The competing demands of special interest groups that focus on major decisions often cancel each other out. A Congressman, for example, might be an Army reservist with a strong tendency toward its doctrine of national strategy which calls for certain types of military preparedness and weaponry; but he would vote for an Air Force appropriation if it meant a factory for his home city; a Navy appropriation if he were rallied by his political leaders on Capitol Hill, and an across-the-board economy cut if he needed to trade a vote with Wilbur Mills, Chairman of the House Ways and Means Committee.

Taking Nothing for Granted

The problem that confronts us is whether we can continue to depend on these countervailing pressures; or whether at some point in our future—nearer than we like to imagine, perhaps—the disparate impulses that go into the military-industrial complex, ranging from a crass desire for profits to honest fear for the safety of the country, may coalesce in such a powerful advocacy of more and better weapons and in such potent opposition to arms control that the entire country will be drawn to support this position.

I am not suggesting that the threat of our industrial-military complex is based in any way on a military-industrial conspiracy. There is no more of a conspiracy here than in numerous other matters where legitimate lobbies influence public policy makers, or where conflicts of interest affect decisions of the legislative and executive arms of government. The free enterprise system is frequently compromised, and political judgments influence every aspect of our national security—but not because of conspiracies. Rather, I am urging that we keep in mind the Eisenhower admonition: "We should take nothing for granted... Only an alert and knowledgeable citizenry can compel the proper meshing of the huge industrial machinery of defense with our peaceful methods and goals, so that security and liberty may prosper together."

1. New York, Dodd, Mead & Company, 1934.
2. *The White House Years,* Vol. II: 1956-1961 *Waging Peace* (New York: Doubleday & Company, Inc., 1965), p. 615.
3. *Ibid.*
4. *UPI* dispatch, January 9, 1968.
5. *The New York Times,* August 8, 1963.
6. Quested in Julius Duscha, *Arms, Money and Politics* (New York: Ives Washburn, Inc., 1965), p. 103.
7. "$30 Billion for Whom?" March 11, 1967, p. 13.

The Usury of War*

Richard F. Kaufman

Richard F. Kaufmann is on the staff of the Subcommittee on Economy in Government, which has investigated profits and costs in defense procurement.

What makes any rational attack on the defense budget so difficult is the extraordinary tenacity of military projects. Old Pentagon "systems" do not die under fire; they merely hibernate, usually in the form of research and development, until a more auspicious day arrives. The symbol of the military-industrial complex is not the octopus—its totem is the phoenix—and what follows here is an attempt to describe its behavior in its Potomac habitat.

Much of the opposition to the Anti-Ballistic Missile System (ABM) is based on the evidence that it probably won't work, is unnecessary, will intensify the arms race, and will divert resources from areas of higher national priority. Unless disproved,

* Richard F. Kaufmann, "The Usury of War," *The Nation* (May 26, 1969), p. 656.

these are good reasons for not spending $6 billion or $7 billion of public money. But rather than respond to the serious arguments, the Pentagon has attempted to cut off debate by revealing one of its "secrets" of the Red Menace—the assertion that Russia's SS-9 missile is intended to be part of a first-strike, offensive threat against the United States. Yet, according to Sen. Stuart Symington, the Senate Armed Services Committee was advised last year that the SS-9 had been built for a second-strike, defensive purpose. The distinction is essential. Unless it can show that the Soviet Union is poised for a first-strike sneak attack, the Pentagon will continue to have a hard time convincing Congress that national security requires an investment in the ABM.

Senator Symington's revelation is one of a number of indications that the time is past when military requests were sacrosanct, at least in some quarters within the legislative branch. A more recent sign in the statement by Sen. Harry Byrd that the facts surrounding the large cost over-run on the C-5A cargo plane have caused him to "view with skepticism the entire military budget" (*Washington Post*, May 2).

One of the clearest expressions thus far of Congressional unhappiness with the level of military spending has been the 1969 Report of the Joint Economic Committee. The report criticizes the President's Council of Economic Advisers and the Economic Report of the President for inadequately analyzing the impact of defense spending, and the Bureau of the Budget for inadequately reviewing Defense Departmnt budget expenses.

In hearings conducted in January and February, the committee heard both Charles J. Zwick and Robert P. Mayo, the outgoing and incoming Budget directors, concede that the bureau does not give as close attention to defense spending as it does to civilian programs. The committee in its report asks whether the defense budget proposed by the Pentagon is seriously questioned elsewhere in the Executive branch. In addition, the committee cites "evidence of widespread waste, mismanagement, and inefficiency in defense spending brought to light in recent months," and comes to this important conclusion: "It now seems clear that the present level of national security can be maintained on a substantially smaller defense budget."

That is the major point of controversy over military spending. Unless the defense budget is cut substantially, the anti-

ABM efforts and other attempts to scrutinize military programs might eventually be regarded as futile. But Congress is at last beginning to question the continued support of a number of major weapons systems, some of which act like aged baseball superstars; they run poorly, can't hit, and are expensive to maintain.

There is some hope that fundamental foreign and military policy assumptions will also be challenged. Perhaps the most basic of these is that the United States must always be armed to fight two major wars and one minor war, simultaneously. Obviously this premise alone has had enormous budgetary implications. If issues of this magnitude are not confronted, and military spending reduced far below the $80 billion (not including defense-related programs and spending for past wars) spent last year, the outcome of fights over more specific issues could be disastrous to the goal of a rational defense program and a manageable military establishment.

For example, the $890 million request for the ABM Safeguard was announced as a reduction from the earlier Sentinel request of $1.8 billion for fiscal year 1970. However, the overall cost of the new Safeguard plan is now estimated at from $6 billion to $7 billion, a sizable increase from the $5 billion price placed on Sentinel. This is called "stretching out" a program. You pay less in a given year, but more in the long run. Indeed, since Safeguard was announced, it has been disclosed that the $6 billion to $7 billion does not include $2 billion for additional research and development, nor $1.2 billion for the nuclear warheads.

Even assuming ABM is curtailed this year, an event that seemed impossible only a few months ago, the total defense budget could end up at about the same level as last year or higher, despite the recent "cuts" announced for fiscal 1970. This could occur by a modification in any one or a combination of other major old and new weapons programs, several of which are actually or potentially more costly than ABM, by requesting additional funds for Vietnam, or by requesting new funds for a new crisis—a Berlin airlift or Cuban missile type of situation. Supplemental appropriations have become routine addenda to the annual budget, including the defense portion. In theory they are caused by unforeseen contingencies; they are also caused by miscalculations of spending requirements. The Pentagon is no doubt already hard at work on a supplemental request for fiscal 1970, to be submitted next fall or early next year. In other words, the budget requests of the Executive branch at the beginning of the year do not tell the full story.

Nor will whatever action is taken on the ABM this year tell the full story, about the ABM or the larger issues inherent in the defense budget. Although it has great implications for the international arms race, the ABM is only one Army weapons system program. The Army, the Navy and the Air Force have other weapons programs, in various stages of design and promotion, that will present problems similar in scope to the ABM. This raises the question alluded to at the start: Do old weapons concepts ever die? Take the case of manned strategic bombers. Ever since the rise of intercontinenal ballistic missiles (ICBMs) after World War II, the bomber has been threatened with extinction. The B-52, built after the Korean War, went into service in 1956. According to the logic of military weaponry, it should have been superseded by a "new generation" of bombers within a few years. The supersonic B-70 was duly chosen as its replacement. Later versions were called the RB-70' and the RS-70. By the end of the Eisenhower administration more than $790 million had been spent on the B-70 program, although additional funds for it had been drastically reduced by the President in 1959.

One of President Kennedy's early acts was to cut requests for B-70 funds in half. They were, however, restored by Congress. Secretary of Defense Robert S. McNamara refused to spend the full amounts appropriated and opposed production and deployment of the new bomber. The basic objection was that it simply made more sense to develop strategic offensive capability through the ICBM than through a manned bomber. But despite McNamara's objections and the eventual defeat of the B-70 and its offspring, the manned supersonic bomber concept has not gone the way of the catapult and trireme. First, instead of being completely eliminated from the budget on the ground that it was a bad idea, the B-70 was continued on a research and development basis. By the time the problem was confronted and the entire B-70 program canceled, one of the prototypes constructed had crashed, and $1.5 billion had been wasted.

Second, the Air Force and its constituency, frustrated by the failure to get a large supersonic plane into full production, began in the early 1960s to promote a commercial version, the supersonic transport (SST). This was a reversal of the usual process, the general experience having been for the government to build large planes for military purposes and for private industry to spin off commercial versions. The classic case was when Boeing built the KC-135 for the Air Force, then used the same basic designs to build the 707 commercial airliner. When the bomber lobby got behind the SST, it was saying, in effect, let the government subsidize this new plane as it has subsidized new planes in the past. Except, this time we will go directly for a subsidized commercial version and spin off the military plane.

For a time in the mid-1960s, Washington must have seemed like heaven for the bomber lobby. Both planes, the B-70 and the SST, were being heavily financed. Then came the termination of the B-70, and a little later President Johnson extended the target date for the SST. However, a final decision was deferred and the program began stretching out. So far, the government has spent almost $500 million on the SST, will probably spend more than a billion on research, development and testing alone. The new budget contains $92.7 million for continued R&D on the program. Efforts are being made to obtain additional funds to build a prototype.

Third, in the middle of the B-70-SST controversy, pressure developed to convert the experimental TFX into a reconnaissance and tactical bomber. The FB-111 resulted, at great cost though without great success. In addition, whereas the public may have thought the B-70 decision had put an end to the ICBM strategic bomber argument, in fact a new design for a supersonic strategic bomber was being worked on. For several years, the Air Force called it the Advanced Manned Strategic Aircraft (AMSA); it has recently been dubbed the B-1A. In 1967, Air Force Secretary Harold Brown admitted to the Senate Committee on Defense Appropriations that the new bomber "is very much like the FB-111." In fact, AMSA is a giant TFX, including the variable (swing) wing. Thus, out of the rubble of the B-70 and the TFX, so to speak, comes AMSA.

Sen. William Proxmire has reported estimates for the new bombers as high as $80 million each. We have at present a force of 646 intercontinental strategic bombers. If we decided to replace only half of them with AMSAs the cost would be $25.8 billion (assuming $80 million each).

Senator Proxmire has stated that the new bomber is unneeded, will be obsolete before it is finished, is a waste of resources, and could heat up the arms race. He also suggests that one of the purposes of AMSA is to provide "backdoor" funds for the SST. In any event, the recently announced cutback of FB-111 purchases, and the new AMSA budget request of $100.2 million, up sharply from last year, to accelerate development, indicates that the bomber lobby is massing for a final breakthrough on a supersonic strategic bomber this year.

The current push for a supersonic strategic bomber can be traced to 1964. By that year, there was no longer hope for deployment of the B-70 or RS-70, although funds to construct three prototype models were requested and spent ($156 million in fiscal 1964). There was a strong belief in government circles that the B-52 would adequately serve our manned strategic bomber needs until it could be phased out in favor of ICBMs. In the face of that belief, the question was whether the government should pour good money into a new bomber design after the $1.5 billion that was being wasted on the B-70.

McNamara supported a $5 million budget request that year "for initial study and development of a manned bomber," but he strongly opposed an additional $50 million that was being urged by the Air Force Chief of Staff, Gen. Curtis E. LeMay. The chairman of the Joint Chiefs of Staff, Gen. Maxwell Taylor, of the Army, was also against it. Responding to a question concerning the phase out of strategic bombers altogether, he told the House subcommittee on Department of Defense Appropriations the same year, "I think the present trend is about right." Not even the Secretary of the Air Force, Eugene Zuckert, supported the request for the additional $50 million. Nevertheless, General Taylor said to the subcommittee: "The emotionally charged decision is one which is going to be faced by the Department of Defense very shortly—that is, whether or not to accept the recommendations of the Air Force with regard to a follow-on bomber."

General LeMay no doubt was shaken, although by no means defeated, by the B-70 fiasco and the widespread resistance to a new bomber. Ever since World War II there had always been new bombers and plans for even newer bombers. Testifying in the 1964 House Appropriations hearings he said: "This is something new for us. We have always replaced our airplanes before we wore them out in the past. As a matter of fact, the B-29s, B-50s, B-36s were all phased out of the inventory at around the 2,000 to 3,000 hour mark."

It must have been difficult for him to understand the opposition to manned bombers by three Presidents, Eisenhower, Kennedy and Johnson. McNamara remained adamantly opposed to the end of his term. As recently as February 1968 he told the Senate Armed Services Committee: "There is no reason in my opinion to move to accept the Air Force proposal, because the national intelligence estimate threat, as presently projected, does not appear to require the AMSA."

Unfortunately, the "emotionally charged decision" was not really faced in 1964 or in the following four years. The bomber lobby kept AMSA alive, as it had the B-70, by obtaining annual R&D funds. The question, to deploy or not to deploy, has never been conclusively answered in public. But the $100.2 million being requested for it this year indicates that the decision has been reached, at least inside the Pentagon. AMSA is rising again.

Defense contractors have played their parts in this birth-death-rebirth drama of the manned supersonic bomber. At present we can only sketch the roles of the key players, without knowing precisely how much each has contributed to the script.

North American Aviation, which has since merged into North American Rockwell, built the airframe for the B-70 prototypes. General Electric built the engines. General Dynamics is the airframe contractor for the TFX and FB-111; Pratt and Whitney, a subsidiary of United Aircraft, builds the engines. On the SST the team is Boeing and GE.

The five are now engaged in a rivalry for AMSA prime contract awards: Boeing, General Dynamics and North American Rockwell for the airframe; GE and Pratt and Whitney for the engines. They are all on the list of the top ten defense contractors for 1968. Together they accounted for $6.5 billion of last year's total military procurement.

How have the Pentagon and the contractors performed on the programs discussed? All we have to go on are the results so far. The B-70 was one of the worst fiascos in recent years. In the 1964 House Appropriations hearings Chairman George Mahon of Texas pointed out that Congress had been "solemnly told that the B-70 would fly long before this date. It has not flown yet." And he concluded: "There has been poor estimating, or poor performance or both." Even General LeMay conceded "that we are disappointed" in the contractors performance.

The TFX has not served the intended purpose of a biservice fighter, and its overall performance is under serious question. The cancellation of the Navy version and the cutback of the FB-111 place the entire multibillion-dollar investment under an even darker cloud than it has been under from its tempestous beginning. The SST seems to be having its troubles. Boeing won the contract on the basis of a variable wing design, then abandoned it in favor of a fixed wing design similar to the losing submission of its rival, Lockheed.

The histories of the ABM and the supersonic strategic bomber contain illuminating parallels. By 1958 the Army had won an inter-service victory over the Air Force for control of the ABM. Earlier the Air Force had tried to develop its own system, called Wizard; the Army called its system the Nike-Zeus, and in 1959 recommended production and deployment. As with the B-70, Eisenhower did not fully support the new weapon, although millions were being spent on research, development and testing.

The magnitude of the resources that would have been wasted had we gone ahead with the Nike-Zeus when the Army wanted it was indicated in the recent, testimony of Dr. George Kistiakowsky, who was Eisenhower's science adviser. Testifying before the Senate Foreign Relations committee last March. Dr. Kistiakowsky said that had the full Nike-Zeus been authorized in 1960, we would have spent "what was then estimated as $20 billion and could have been, judging by analogy with other large weapons systems, twice as much," and that it would now be obsolete.

As with the B-70 and AMSA, there have been deep reservations and strong resistance to ABM in the highest government cycles, including Presidential and Cabinet levels. McNamara opposed it until his last year in office. In 1964, after Nike-Zeus had been abandoned in favor of Nike-X, he estimated that a

Nike-X program would cost $16 billion, not including annual costs of operation. He added that his figure might be too low, that the program might have to be considerably expanded for defense against a large Soviet attack, and that before investing in it we should carefully consider the costs of additional programs that would be required once we went ahead with ABM. The civil defense program would have to be substantially expanded to protect against the effects of enemy missiles and our own ABM missiles; an expanded fallout shelter program would cost about $800 million, McNamara estimated in 1967. Improving our bomber defenses to protect the ABM would bring additional costs, estimated from $1.5 to $2.4 billion.

Thus, due to reservations and resistance based on evidence of past failures and an unfavorable cost-effectiveness ratio, the decision to produce and deploy was deferred from year to year, while funding for further R&D and testing was allowed to continue. In this way, the ABM has dragged on for more than a decade.

The prime contracts for Nike-Zeus and Nike-X, the earlier ABM systems, were awarded to Western Electric, a subsidiary of AT&T, also one of the top ten defense contractors. Actually, the Army's relationship with Western Electric goes back before Nike-Zeus at least to 1945 when the Army selected it as the Nike anti-aircraft program manager. Western Electric is also the prime contractor for the Safeguard system.

In 1964 the Permanent Subcommittee on Investigations, headed by Sen. John L. McClellan, issued a report containing a devastating analysis of the Army-Western Electric relationship throughout the Nike programs. The report is entitled "Pyramiding of Profits and Costs in the Missile Procurement Program." It shows, among other things, how Western Electric managed to make millions of dollars in excess profits by obtaining fees from the government for jobs on which it did absolutely no work. Western Electric's major subcontractor, Douglas Aircraft Co. (now merged into McDonnell-Douglas, another of the top ten contractors), did the same thing.

For example, on one contract (for launcher loaders) Western Electric sent to the Army invoices totaling $16.4 million, including its profit of $955,396. In fact, Western Electric had incurred direct costs of only $14,293 on that contract, for "checking over the launcher loaders." The bulk of the $16.4 million was identified as the price paid by Western Electric to its subcontractor, Douglas. Thus Western Electric was able to parlay its $14,293 worth of effort on this one contract into $955,396, or a profit of 6,684 per cent. On another contract (for trailers), Western Electric was two steps removed from actual production, yet managed to add a $3.2 million profit for itself to the government's bill.

An analysis of Western Electric's financial reports for the ten-year period 1951 through 1960 shows an extraordinary jump in its profits with the increase in Nike sales. In 1951 Western Electric's government sales totaled 12.8 per cent of its business. Nike sales were relatively low that year, and the company's return on net investment for its government business was only 12.1 per cent. By the following year, Nike sales had picked up and so had Western Electric's profits on government business. For 1952, government sales rose to 24.4 per cent of its business, and return on investment increased to 27.7 percent. For the ten-year period, government sales averaged 26.6 per cent of Western Electric's business: return on investment averaged 28.3 per cent on its government work.

The McClellan subcommittee concluded that Western Electric had taken large unearned profits out of the Nike programs. In addition, it reprimanded the Army for its inept administration. The Army ignored a government auditor's warning that unreasonable profits were being charged. It permitted its own technical competence to deteriorate so badly that it became dependent on contractors like Western Electric. The report contains the following conclusion: "Knowing that the Army lacked the capability to manage the system, Western Electric refused to maintain responsibility for systems integrity unless all Nike parts were bought through them. They gave one concession, permitting the Army to procure, elsewhere, standard items such as screwdrivers, pliers, antifreeze, and paper cups."

The report, by the way, also criticizes Boeing for taking excess profits in the Air Force's Bomarc missile program (part of SAGE, our bomber defense system), and General Dynamics for doing the same in the Titan missile program. Boeing beefed up its profits in two ways, by playing the profit pyramiding game and by overestimating its costs during contract negotiations with the government so as to increase its profits under the incentive contract provisions.

The ABM and AMSA are both built on foundations of adverse experiences. Their survival, or disinterment, is a tribute to the persistence of their purveyors. How much else lies buried in the defense budget? Too much. It is as if a vast subcontinent were filled with the buried treasures of a dozen Captain Kidds and their crews. If one were to read the defense budget like a treasure map one could recognize the telltale signs of perhaps a score of other multibillion-dollar weapons systems, stashed away in various stages of development and production.

To name a few, in addition to ABM and AMSA, there are MIRV (multiple independently targeted re-entry vehicle for nuclear missiles), Minuteman III (replacement for Minuteman I and Minuteman II ICBMs), MOL (manned orbiting lab), Poseidon (replacement for Polaris nuclear submarine missiles), AWACS (airborne warning and control system), C-5A (huge cargo plane), F-14 (new Navy fighter plane) and F-15 (new Air Force fighter plane). Numerous other programs, whose eventual costs are secret, occasionally come to the surface because of investigation by Congress or through the press. Examples are the Sanguine program in Wisconsin and chemical and biological warfare projects, such as the one that killed more than 6,000 sheep near the Dugway Proving Grounds, Utah, in 1968. And the public gets glimpses of other programs from time to time when it suits the Defense Department's purposes. The eventual costs are unknown because they are all still in the R&D stage. Examples recently made known by the Pentagon are laser-guided bombs, TV-guided bombs and missiles, a Navy shipboard missile defense system, and a ship- and air-launched anti-ship missile.

The point here is that it is difficult if not impossible to keep track of every scheme to find money for every weapons system and anti-weapons system from the time it may be only a gleam in a contractor's eye through its conception, nurture, growth and delivery. Occasionally, a large program like the ABM will appear to be so ill conceived that a campaign specifically to defeat it will be necessary. But the fact is that even if ABM is significantly retarded this year, the great effort that has gone into the anti-ABM campaign would probably have to be duplicated again and again. The Army will not sit still while its service rivals get the big, prestigious weapons systems, and the Army's contractors will not sit idle while its competitors get the more lucrative contracts. For these reasons, the most effective approach to control over military spending, in addition to fighting the more ominous and ludicrous individual programs, is to reduce the level of military spending by a significant amount. Senator Proxmire and others in the Senate and House have recommended a $10 billion cut this year. Sen. Allen J. Ellender recently expressed the growing concern over the defense budget when he stated: "I think this year it is going to become much more obvious to the Congress and public how much more tremendous level of Pentagon spending is costing the nation in relation to our other needs. This is the primary reason I am so opposed to the commitment of vast sums of money to the development of military hardware, which all too often becomes obsolete before it is ever operational. It is a waste, a gigantic waste, and it detracts from the scale of our national life."

The sheer inefficiency of defense management and defense production, as demonstrated by such recent fiascos as the TFX, the C-5A, and the Sheridan-Shillelagh tank, more than justifies this kind of statement. With less money to play around with, the Pentagon might possibly impose a greater sense of responsibility upon itself and encourage the defense industry to do the same. Efficiency, of course, is not the single nor even the main issue. Rationality, balance and civility are at stake in the current struggle over the size of the defense budget. That is why the real question may be not *when*, but *whether*, demobilization is possible.

The Military-Industrial Complex — A Perspective*

Eugene M. Zuckert

Eugene M. Zuckert served as Secretary of the Air Force from 19   to 19 , serving longer in that office than any other individual.

For twenty-five years I worked in a variety of capacities to help build a proper and productive relationship between government and industry— a relationship necessary to meet the needs of our national defense. Today I am saddened. That relationship has been misunderstood, has been criticized, has been denigrated, and the term "military-industrial complex" has been used as a mark of opprobrium. This has been true even though it took the same skills and the same resources of the very same complex to produce the much-applauded Apollo 11!

How and why has this come about?

What I hope to do this evening is to give you some views, based on my own experience, what I believe lies behind the public controversy which now pours more heat than light on the problems of our national defense and defense establishment.

I am proud of the Defense Establishment of today, that I have had some share in building it to its present level of effectiveness. But, at the same time, I am not blind to the faults, the failings and the built-in inefficiencies that one can find in the Defense Establishment or in any huge organization, particularly one which does not have to sell its products to the public to stay in business.

I have spent a good part of a lifetime looking for those faults and for ways to correct them. I only wish that the current critics of the Defense Establishment were looking sincerely for genuine faults and positive corrections. But basically, that is not at all what the most vocal of the critics are after.

---

* Eugene M. Zuckert, "The Military-Industrial Complex — A Perspective." Speech given before the Defense and Contract Procurement Administration Conference, Washington, D.C.

What is the thread of the allegations against the military and its supporting industry? It goes far beyond a concern for the proper level of military expenditures. There is an underlying charge that a conspiracy exists among our military and the defense industry that results in wasteful spending for arms with consequent profits to industry and an inordinately swollen military posture. From that running start, the charges fan out and derive nourishment from sensationalized treatment of a variety of examples of mistakes and inefficiencies, real or alleged.

At the same time, a whole host of newly qualified military experts spring up on all sides; there is a startling discovery that the military has run wild because of perfunctory scrutiny of the defense budget. That is particularly ironical to me because I recall the vigorous McNamara budget process. The fashionable criticism in those days was that our military suffered an excess of civilian control with a resulting downgrading of experienced military judgment.

It is my considered judgment that the current furor over the military industrial complex is really an attack on an unpopular war. Wasn't it Arnold Toynbee, the great historian, who said that war weariness is a most useful tool for dictators and demagogues? The critics of the Vietnam war have been raging on the Potomac since 1965, and they are not likely to subside soon. The professors, politicians and pundits who are already in the fray are enjoying it immensely, and they have friends who also are bound to claim "a piece of the action."

There is a long list of things which the storm over the military industrial complex is not:

It is *not*—as advertised—a Great Debate over American Defense and Foreign Policy. A Great Debate, in my opinion, is desperately needed. But this isn't it.

It is *not*—as some claim—a popular uprising against militarism and procurement hanky-panky in the Pentagon. Waste there is and always will be. But these critics are opposed to the Defense Establishment no matter how well run.

Nor is it—as claimed—a "concerned dialogue" over national priorities. How can you have a "dialogue" on whether we should have obsolete weapons systems or higher vertical slums? The two serious problems deserve serious attention, not rhetorical flim-flam.

What we're experiencing is not even a rational discussion of the weapons systems our current national defense posture requires. One cannot find in all the arguments an effort to define our needs and then measure the Defense Establishment against the requirements.

Superficially, the controversy over the military-industrial complex might seem to arise from any or all of these issues, depending on what syndicated column or Washington newsletter you read.

But don't you believe it. All the sloganeering just doesn't add up: How we must reassess our national priorities by cutting back our defense expenditures; how we have to get the military under civilian control: how we are headed down the road to militarism and fascism.

The controversy over the military industrial complex is the same tired old combination of *unilateral disarmament* and pious hopes that we have seen played on the Washington circuit off and on for well over a quarter of a century! The young ones don't know it, and the old ones too often have forgotten, but we've seen and heard it all before.

To be sure the format has been updated. Now it's a kind of ideological Western. The military industrial complex is cast in the role of the bad guys. Forty years ago it was the "Merchants of Death" — but the plot was the same.

All reasonable persons can applaud conscientious dispassionate inquiry into and search for evidence of stupidity, incompetence, favoritism and waste in military procurement. Responding to such inquiries is a legitimate part of the job for the uniformed and civilian Defense leaders who must defend their management before Congress.

The cost of the C5A transport or blunders on the Cheyenne helicopter and the effectiveness of the supertank — these are all appropriate subjects for Congressional investigation by the able committees charged with that responsibility.

But what I regard as dangerous and illegitimate is the highly organized and furiously pressed propaganda assault on our defense institutions disguised as a selfless effort by "concerned" intellectuals to have the nation from takeover by an alleged combination of defense industry profiteers and a war-minded military.

Some there are who may say this merely is symptomatic of the malaise of our times — part of the current attack on so many of our established traditions and institutions. Some there are who will insist that a better-educated and more enlightened populace has finally risen in righteous wrath and indignation against a longtime evil.

Actually, however, the scenario is old hat.

It was first staged in the early '30s by a curious combination of far-out Liberal intellectuals and a group of Republican isolationist Senators of that era. The isolationist Senators just did not want the United States in any more European wars. Some of the involved intellectuals believed that the French and British were about to join with Hitler in common cause against Russian communism. But whatever the motivations, and they were mixed, everybody in the combination wanted to make sure that Wall Street and the munitions-makers of World War I were blamed for whatever past, present or future problems could be claimed.

So what played the Washington circuit then was a truly memorable extravaganza. A Senate Committee (to become famous as the Nye Committee) set out to investigate the relationship between Wall Street and American War profiteers and munitionsmakers who stood accused of having dragged the United States into World War I. The production played to standing room only. It received tremendous publicity and developed a new "devil image" for Wall Street and American Big Business, the evil.

Congress rushed to pass the Neutrality Act of 1935. Free from the machination of the Merchants of Death, we were all, presumably, safe.

Sure we were — until the roof caved in on us at Pearl Harbor.

Today, many of the players are different. But the archvillain is the same — something called this time the military-industrial complex.

But what the nation could endure in the peaceful, non-nuclear '30s becomes an irrational luxury in the nuclear, cold war '60s. We can see the danger now that a colossal demonstration of pacifist sentiment may well lead to hasty and ill-advised actions designed to fetter our defense establishment and impair our defense posture. This, in turn, could be misread as a sign of our weakness, and it could trigger the very confrontation that the anti-military group presumably wants to avoid.

Does this sound far-fetched? I don't think so. Let's look at what happened in the '40s, the '50s, as a result of so-called "popular demand":

Remember the frantic demobilization of our fighting forces and the defense industry we had built to meet the needs of World War II? We paid heavily for that spasmodic reflex to strident, fomented hysteria. I had a ringside seat at the anti-military fights that went on before, during and after that struggle. (I was then Special Assistant to Stuart Symington, Assistant Secretary of War for Air.) The critics hastily cut the armed forces and just as hastily rebuilt them for Korea.

In 1949 I watched the late Defense Secretary, Louis Johnson — acting under Presidential orders to economize — cut the military budget to the bone. That was the year when Russia developed her own A-bomb, on which *we* were supposed to have a monopoly for at least twenty years!

It took the communist invasion of Korea in 1950 to teach us the hard way that the ill-considered demobilization and disarmament after World War II was a disaster never again to be invited.

That's when we started, painfully and expensively, to rebuild the defense establishment we had deliberately and ruthlessly wrecked.

The furious controversy over our development of nuclear and thermonuclear weapons compounded the difficulties of recapturing and rebuilding our initiative in nuclear technology. This was brought home to me when I served as an Atomic Energy Commission member from 1952 to 1954.

I went back to the Pentagon in January of 1961 as Secretary of the Air Force under a truly great Secretary of Defense— Robert S. McNamara. During that tour of duty, in the Administrations of Presidents Kennedy and Johnson, I saw the Defense Establishment revitalized in muscle and posture.

There was a sharp break with former Treasury Secretary Humphrey's insistence that a balanced national budget must be accorded priority over the requirements of national security.

A defense policy based on the Dulles doctrine of massive

retaliation was replaced with President Kennedy's posture of "flexible response" to aggression.

He made a unique contribution of great permanent significance in substantially improving the quality of information that forms the basis of the decision process in the Pentagon.

And probably most important, Secretary McNamara made giant strides toward the nation's goal of actually unifying the missions of our armed forces which the Unification Act, as amended in 1958, called for.

Secretary McNamara put together a defense establishment under civilian control of which the nation can be proud. And he established the elements of the sound and proper relationship between our military leadership and the nation's defense industry which I devoutly hope will endure in the years ahead.

This is only part of what is being threatened today.

In Vietnam our soldiers fight in a war that could well be won for the enemy on the propaganda front at home. Right here.

In the new concept of revolutionary warfare—between an open society like ours and the closed systems of Russia, China and North Vietnam—our public opinion environment becomes the decisive battlegrounds. Both Ho Chi Minh and General Giap have repeatedly declared that the propaganda front of American public opinion will be the theater of the final and decisive communist victory in the Vietnam War. You may be sure they have taken great care to secure Hanoi's homefront against the kind of disruptive tactics which are a daily occurrence here.

In North Vietnam, offenses such as "disrupting public order," speaking against the war, staging student demonstrations or "undermining the solidarity of the people" draw penalties ranging up to life imprisonment and death.

None of us would want to see any of our freedoms so constrained. We must use self-restraint as we exercise our hard-won rights of free speech. And we must face realities. We must understand that a major war goal for Ho Chi Minh and General Giap is a psychological one—the dramatic and enduring humiliation of the United States with a significant influence on the shadow and substance of American power, particularly in Asia.

For the President (any President) and the Senate (any Senate) Vietnam presents an issue of American foreign policy which will *not* be solved simply by bringing our troops home in a blind rush.

Vietnam is a test of the Truman Doctrine, established in 1947 by a Democratic President with the solid approval of the Republican 80th Congress. A defeat for the policy in Vietnam will invite similar challenges elsewhere.

These are strange times indeed. The Democratic party seems to be abandoning the Truman Doctrine. The stance of many of it leaders in the fight against deployment of an ABM carried overtones of a reversion to the Dulles policy of "massive retaliation." Some of the Liberal intellectual rhetoric sounds like an echo of the old arch-conservative rallying cry of "Fortress America."

I don't get it.

One thing I do get. Inevitably and unavoidably, in the absence of clearly defined policies or clairvoyance of the future, the military establishment must plan to fight almost every kind of war that could be thrust upon us.

Another anomaly. So many ardent supporters of the late President Kennedy are now enthusiastic participants in the campaign against the Vietnam War and the offshoot crusade against the military industrial complex. Have they forgotten the words of President Kennedy in his Inaugural Address? He said:

"We dare not tempt them with weakness. For only when our arms are sufficient beyond doubt can we be certain beyond doubt that they will never be employed."

I haven't forgotten. . .

What Eisenhower Really Said*

Navy Magazine

When the tough old soldier finally succumbed at 79 after an unprecedented number of heart attacks and other illnesses, the

---

* "What Eisenhower Really Said," *Navy Magazine*.

nation lost one of the greatest and certainly the best loved leader of our age. We still leave to history a detailed appraisal of Dwight D. Eisenhower's record as Allied Commander in Europe in World War II and as President of the United States. He had his critics during both periods, particularly as President. But if he failed to do some things some people feel he should have done, Ike unquestionably was victorious in war and successful in keeping the United States prosperous, strong and at peace during his years in the White House.

His breadth of view was well known. He coined the term "parochial" for those military leaders and others who judge things only by partisan or preconceived concepts. Although a West Pointer, General Eisenhower immediately saw the tremendous advantages of the Polaris submarine and a nuclear power surface Navy and pushed such developments more than any other President. He backed aircraft carriers and strategic air and missile power, often to the dismay of the Army. We say no more about the late former Commander-in-Chief for two reasons. NAVY published a full length article about him in March. And we feel the urgent need to comment on a current movement which uses another term he coined.

We refer to the powerful current of antimilitarism that is sweeping the country which blames "the military-industrial complex" for most of our current ills. In his farewell address as President, Ike warned against the *potential* danger of large armed forces and a huge arms industry gaining "unwarranted influence" in our nation, while at the same time stressing that both were "vital" to our survival.

The phrase, quoted completely out of context, has become the catch-word, the spearhead of an attack against anything concerned with maintaining an adequate U.S. national defense and almost everything America has stood for. Not only the militant radicals, but respected liberal Senators, editors, columnists, commentators, scientists and professors have used the phrase as "proof" that not only should defense spending be drastically cut to add billions immediately to solve the real problems of poverty and the cities, but also in support of anything they personally oppose concerning the military. They lose sight of the totally important factors of military strength needed to preserve the Republic.

These sophisticated leaders of American thought—who are quick to accuse others of the crime of lifting statements out of context—use the bare phase or a sentence or two of Eisenhower's comment in a way that undoubtedly would distress him if he were here. The alleged "military-industrial complex" is cited constantly as a reason to vote down the ABM, new warships, planes, and other proposed weapons systems. The term appears in every argument for abandoning the ROTC, military research at universities, barring military or defense industry recruiters from campuses, ending the draft and in favor of any number of unilateral disarmament proposals, pulling out of Viet Nam without honor and turning the other cheek at whatever North Viet Nam does to us.

Eisenhower's oft-quoted warning about the dangers of a combination of large armed forces and a big defense industry did indeed warn of the "potential for the disastrous rise of misplaced power" which could endanger American liberties and democratic processes.

But this was only a small part of what he said in a speech primarily concerned with his great desire to maintain peace. He warned against the danger of global Communism, and then said:

"A vital element in keeping the peace is our military establishment. Our arms must be mighty, ready for instant action, so that no potential aggressor may be tempted to risk his own destruction."

He noted that the U.S. military organization and American industry had greatly changed since pre-World War II days, when we had no armaments industry and when "American makers of plowshares could, with time and as required, make swords as well."

"But now," he added, "we can no longer risk emergency improvisation of national defense; we have been compelled to create a permanent armaments industry of vast proportions" and a 3.5 million man military establishment. His warning against the "potential" of a "military-industrial complex" gaining "unwarranted influence" and endangering "our liberties or democratic processes" followed.

What Life magazine called the current "highly emotional general attack on the U.S. military establishment" has stimulated new Congressional investigations into Pentagon "waste" and charges that the "military" has dominated U.S. foreign policy, overcommitting the nation around the world. There has indeed been "waste" in that a number of weapons systems have been cancelled either because they failed to measure up to standards, were outmoded before they were ready, or were late and costs ran up and performance improvement proved marginal. But war is waste, and this is the nature of the game. Pentagon decision-makers must agonize between chancing mistakes on risky new weapons with great promise or catastrophe if they wait until the other side achieves some technological breakthrough that would leave the United States open to attack. Russia has been building a new prototype fighter plane almost every year and scrapping it in favor of a new model. All nations always have done the same thing with the same results and the same charges of "waste." Some of it could have been avoided, and top military officers must bear a share of the blame.

But it is important to note that civilian leaders, not only in the Pentagon but also in the White House and State Department, for the past eight years, have made the major decisions on weapons systems and strategy — not the uniformed leaders who are getting the most criticism. They did not make the decisions on major strategy in the Viet Nam War, on the Bay of Pigs, in the Cuban Crisis, or in leaving the Northwestern Pacific so unguarded as to make the *Pueblo* and EC-121 incidents possible.

Military officers, unhappy at being the targets of recent attacks, resent even more the fact that General David M. Shoup, retired Commandant of the Marine Corps, and long a military maverick, joined the assailers with a vitriolic attack on the officers corps as the leaders of the "military-industry complex" in an article in Atlantic magazine. He accused many of them, in effect, of being "war lovers." Another retired Marine officer, Colonel Robert Heinl, now military analyst of the Detroit News, accuses Shoup of "going sour" on his profession and country because of frustrated "political ambitions" and a "desire for publicity."

The origins of the present attack on the military are clear. General Earle G. Wheeler, chairman of the Joint Chiefs of Staff, blames it on "frustration" against the Viet Nam War, which "has gone on so long," with no clearcut outcome, along with a rejection by many Americans of our involvement in "other nations' security affairs" in unpopular wars like Korea and Viet Nam, as well as the huge cost of new weapons.

There is no question but that U.S. military policy and force levels are in for a thorough reexamination. But this can have its good side. In reviewing overseas commitments including the maintenance of many divisions and air units in Europe, which Mr. Eisenhower criticized, Congress can take a good look at alternate and more economical strategies, such as the seabased one. But, looking back on history, we are concerned lest the new wave of antimilitarism gets out of hand. We recall the fervent belief in the '20s of the Kellogg Treaty solemnly outlawing war. And how Senator Gerald Nye, and his Subcommittee Counsel, Alger Hiss, almost convinced the American people, in a highly publicized Congressional investigation, that the "merchants of death" (munitions makers) were largely responsible for wars, causing many Americans to ignore Hitler and other aggressors. Somehow, the current attack on the "military-industrial complex" smacks of the Nye-Hiss "merchants of death" campaign of the '30s which almost left America unguarded when World War II came.

Chapter Three

The Military and the Campus

Traditionally, the University has had only an indirect role in the great issues of American political life. Certainly the concepts taught in the classroom, the research done in the laboratories and the moral and intellectual influences of faculty and administrators has helped to shape emerging economic, social, and political trends. But since the University was seen primarily as a place where the dispassionate search for truth could be carried on unmolested by the work-a-day world, the participation of faculty members and administrators in political causes was accomplished through their roles as concerned citizens and through other institutions. This traditional view of the University has been swept aside, as have so many other traditional beliefs by the events of the past decade.

The University, whether for good or for evil, is now drawn directly into the caldron of political turmoil. First the civil rights movement, then the black power movement, and most recently the ecology movement have all forced universities as institutions to choose sides. Involvement, not detachment, is the watchword of the lay. But no event has stunned the campuses across the nation more profoundly than the Vietnamese war. No issue has so sharply polarized American students; no issue has transformed thousands of apolitical and nonpolitical students into intense militants with but one thought: end the war.

The militants argue that they have exhausted the resources of the American political system; their efforts have brought no change. Nor is there, they argue, any prospect that change will occur in the future unless the intensity of their resistance to the war is communicated to the establishment through violence. Hence, they have turned from precinct work to harrassment of recruiters from Dow Chemical, from signing petitions to sit-ins in Dean's offices, and from writing congressmen to liberation of buildings. They have made the campus their battleground and they have strongly resisted all efforts to still their voices.

In this continuing struggle against the University, which the militants assert is a corrupt institution in a corrupt society, two targets have been particularly attractive: the Reserve Officers Training programs and classified military related research on campus. Both of these are attractive targets because they are directly related to the military, they generally have an identifiable physical home which makes an inviting target for rocks and fire bombs, and they have lost to a considerable extent the traditional support which they enjoyed. Directly related to the military, easily identifiable, and isolated, both of these programs have fought a rear guard action to protect their positions on campus. ROTC has been easily the most vulnerable target. Even on those campuses where administrators and faculty have been unwilling to force the program to close completely, there has been much support for depriving ROTC programs of academic credit, placing them on an extracurricular basis and denying faculty status to ROTC instructors. These acts have been accompanied by much sneering at the academic content of the courses and the competence level of the instructors.

The readings in this section were chosen to highlight the issues involved in this debate. It is a debate which generates more heat than most, and which raises issues that run to the heart of the question which must ultimately be answered: What role for the American University?

ROTC: The Lower Learning*

Milton Mayer

Milton Mayer is a member of the faculty of the University of Massachusetts in Amherst. He has also taught at the University of Chicago, Frankfurt University, and the Comenius Theological Faculty of Prague.

It was quiz night in Sophomore English. My moppets had their little beaks in the *Iliad*, and the classroom was quiet. I sat there scratching my sores and tutelarily wondering if college students still wondered what they were supposed to "get" out of five hundred pages of barbarous battlecries, hideous warwhoops, and rebel yells. The silence was suddenly rent (as Homer would say) by barbarous battle-cries, hideous warwhoops, and rebel yells from somewhere inside the building; and just as suddenly restored. It was as if we had touched down on the plain of Troy and then taken off again.

The next morning I received a call from Major Veepings of the Reserve Officers' Training Corps, who asked if he might speak with me. I told him that I was at his armed service, and he said: "Professor Mayer, I want to apologize on behalf of the ROTC for the disturbance in the building last night, and to ask if it would be possible for you to find another building for your evening class. You see, sir, we have a Counterinsurgency course on Tuesday evenings, and Colonel Murgatroyd is afraid that some of your students might misunderstand what is going on." ("You mean," I said to myself, "understand.")

I told the Major that I would withdraw my forces, thanked him for the use of the barracks, and decided to do something I had not done for going on fifty years, namely, think about ROTC (or Rot-cee, as the kids call it).

What I had thought about Rot-cee going on fifty years ago wasn't flattering. Unpossessed of the martial virtues, I repre-

---

* Milton Mayer, "ROTC: The Lower Learning," *The Progressive* (December 1968) p. 16.

hended them. Besides, the country I grew up in was not a martial country. In those days, the statutory quota of 100,000 was the large standing army which President Washington had opposed as "dangerous to our liberties." But the recruiters on Skid Row could not find anything like 100,000 end-of-the-line derelicts to fill the quota. In the Preparedness campaign of 1916 the Secretary of what was then called War had to appeal to restaurants to remove their No SOLDIERS ADMITTED signs.

After the defeat of Kaiser Bill the citizen army (average schooling: four years) was demobilized. But the dying echoes persisted into the early 1920s. When I reached high school in 1921 the ROTC was attracting the filling-station set of the future; a few years later, not even them. When I entered the University of Chicago in 1925 everybody who was anybody was kicking it. (Chicago had never let it in.) The immigrant hatred of "European militarism seemed to have survived the raptures of the Great War.

World War II was strictly business. By 1943 the colleges and universities were wholly converted to war training, war research, and war production. Kill-or-die for real put the kibosh on Rot-cee. But in 1948 the United States of America adopted peacetime conscription (which Woodrow Wilson had called "the root evil of Prussianism"). ROTC immediately revived, with an instant correlation between enrollment and the Berlin airlift, Korea, and the Cuban missile crisis. Vietnam sent it soaring. "Increasing draft calls motivate additional men to apply to ROTC," says the commandant at Berkeley, where enrollment leapt from 253 to 795 during the great escalation of 1965-66. Last spring, with graduate students callable under the new draft regulations, many units reported a 100 per cent increase in applications.

If, in the 1950s, you did not especially want to canoe the Yalu River or, in the 1960s, explore the Mekong Delta, and you could not pass a science course, you enrolled in Military Science and got a guaranteed deferment. It was axiomatic (as it still is) that you could not flunk Military Science; an axiom supported by the Army's own advertisement that its six-week summer training camp "takes the place of the two-year ROTC Basic Course." If you hup-hup for two years, and then sign on for two years more of five fifty-minute periods a week, you can hardly miss an ROTC Scholarship which pays your tuition, books, and laboratory expenses, and $50 a month besides.

This doesn't mean that your mother raised her boy to be a soldier; on the contrary, it means a fighting chance of not fighting. In 1962, the compulsory ROTC programs (which forty per cent of the students always found one way or another of ducking) had a seventy per cent dropout after the required two years. Not now; four years of being fired at with blanks by college chums has a certain contemporary charm. Draft-age patriots would rather be red, white, or blue than dead.

The once high hope of getting rid of Rot-cee has gone glimmering. As a better 'ole than Vietnam it is cemented into the campuses of 250 colleges and universities across the country. It has, of course, no more to do with the higher learning than it ever had. It has to do with marching up the hill, and, if you haven't had your head shot off at the top, down again. It does not produce good officers, because virtue is not absorbed through the soles of the feet. The only way the Army — any Army — can get good men to be trained as officers is to dragoon them. And this it can't do on the campus. Beginning in 1923 (when the University of Wisconsin threw it out) compulsory ROTC faded from all of the better (and most of the worse) institutions at the rate of twelve units a year. It faded fighting, though, until, the attrition unabating, the Army finally "approved of" voluntary programs in spite of the fact that the changeover means an instantaneous drop of never less than eighty per cent of the enrollment. Two years before the compulsory program was dropped by the University of Massachusetts in 1962, it was opposed in a student survey by seventy-five per cent of the males *and by ninety per cent of the conscript cadets.* In wartime 1942, eighty per cent of the draftees selected for Officer Candidate School were college graduates; less than six per cent of them were Rot-cee products.

Sixty-one of the ROTC units — the big ones — are in the land-grant colleges, established by the Morrill Act with Federal funds derived from the sale of the Western lands. The wholesome purpose was instruction in the agricultural and mechanical arts. But there was a war on at the time — the time was 1862 —

and the new cow colleges were required to offer a course in "military science and tactics." It was under this requirement that Rot-cee was born in 1916.

In time many of the land-grant schools became state universities. Most of them (and all of the best of them) no longer require ROTC. But there is no getting rid of it altogether; under the land-grant act they have to offer it. And such anguish as they may harbor is assuaged by the money that's in it. The ROTC Vitalization Act of 1964 *doubled* the scholarship funds of one state university. The money would seem to be wasted, at least in peacetime; of 2,000 lieutenants commissioned at the University of California in Los Angeles, only 200 have chosen a military career. Only in total war, when the Army Reserve is sent into combat, is there a possible payoff; but the total wars have to be no more than ten years apart or the boys who won their spurs in Rot-cee will be as archaic as the spurs.

For the students, the come-on, aside from postponement of that trip to the no longer Mysterious East, is the counting of ROTC credits toward graduation. Faculties generally despise the program, except for the A.&M.-phys-ed-campus-police amalgam and an occasional Army man in the natural sciences. Where academic bodies have the opportunity (as they did at Boston University this spring), they strip it of its credits, reducing its positive student appeal to the money they get if they stick it out. Occasional professors of engineering, looking for scholarships for their fledglings, fancy the Army's magnanimous grants for advanced training, but the Engineering Council for Professional Development strenuously opposes Rot-cee credits toward an engineering degree. . . .

President Asa S. Knowles of Northeastern University, a private institution in Massachusetts, is ROTC's academic showpiece. Addressing a recent meeting of newly appointed Rot-cee instructors, he said, "You must be prepared to face intellectual hostility. The war in Vietnam is not a popular war. There are many Americans who oppose our involvement in it. Many of these people may be found on the college campus. Whether they speak out of ignorance, sincere disagreement, or are merely parroting the ideas of others, the fact remains that they have a right to speak. The college campus is no military reservation

... You must expect to have to defend your beliefs in the face of learned opponents. ... The recitation of pat answers will fall on deaf ears. Appeals to patriotism are virtually meaningless. I do not mean to suggest that I condone this situation. I merely wish to inform you that it exists. ..."

What President Knowles failed to account for was the intellectual hostility of these unpatriotic parrots *before* Vietnam — an hostility greatly exacerbated, but only exacerbated, by the war. Rot-cee may not be the only non-intellectual program on the campus, but it is the only one that is, by universal and traditional definition, anti-intellectual. Last year a subcommittee appointed to investigate ROTC reported to the Faculty Senate of one land-grant institution that "the law and political realities preclude a decision that ROTC has no place on the campus." Members of the Senate's Academic Matters Committee "generally sensed that somehow the military was different, not a part of the academic family," and the subcommittee expressed its "doubts concerning the quality of the program, quality of instruction, and quality of educational material."

War, though it may not be a liberal art, is an art, and like all arts is acquired on the job. The place to learn soldiering is the Army. Rot-cee is a pale imitation of the Army, and a still paler imitation of the job on the battlefield. If, however, the essence of soldiering is drill, drill, and more drill, Rot-cee has its use, all the way from about-face to "Operation of Telephones and Switchboards." In Military Science I, the Leadership Laboratory Program includes Squad Drill, Platoon Drill, Company Drill, Mass Drill, Review of Drill, Manual of Arms, Practice for Fall and Spring Review, and Fall and Spring Review; all told, fourteen hours out of thirty. In MS II, Leadership Laboratory includes all the drill all over again, plus Saber Manual and Command Voice. (Obey Voice does not appear in the curriculum.) ...

Rot-cee is not content to teach young men how to crack other young men's heads. They have to crack their own in the program's "academic" courses — those for which the Army is most insistent that the college or university give credit toward graduation. These courses are preeminently three in number, *American Military History, The United States Army and National*

Security, and *The Role of the United States in World Affairs.*
(The last in particular drives historians and political scientists
up the wall.)

The competence of the men who teach these "academic" subjects is determined by the Army, not by the college or the university (which may reject an Army appointee, but almost never
does in practice; and in any case finally has to accept one). If he
is the commandant of the unit, the Army contract requires the
institution to give him a full professorship.

His fellow professors have him cornered on the campus,
and he can't get at them. What he can get at is the cadet who
doesn't have the Rot-cee spirit. A major at Berkeley is telling
his charges about SLAM, a Mach 3 missile with a cruising alti-
tude of 50-100 feet. "Even if it misses its target," he says, "the
sonic boom it creates will kill enough people to make it worth
while." Some of his students are looking at him hard-eyed —
or he thinks they are. "The Air Force," he goes on, "has broken
the sound barrier and the heat barrier and is tackling the speed
of light." More gas-light glares. "In spite of Einstein and his
theories our boys are working out ways to fly twice, three times
the speed of sound." Audible snickers now. "Go ahead and laugh,
but those that do will some day be marching to the goose-step
and tune of the hammer and sickle."

But the student who really wants to take Rot-cee is not generally of the snickering sort. "We don't have radicals in the
ROTC," says a major on one of the country's more radical campuses, Wisconsin. "There are obnoxious elements here." — For
the past ten years the Anti-Military Ball at Madison has been
outdrawing the Military Ball on the same night.—"They laugh at
the flag-wavers, but what we need is more flag-waving." The
future flag-wavers (with, in the event, at least one obnoxious
element in their midst) enter a classroom and are told not to take
notes and not to tell anyone what they are about to see. What
they are about to see—this at the University of Washington—is
a series of three slide pictures. The first is a map of the U.S. West
Coast with red dots marking the major cities and towns; the
second an identification of the red dots as chapter headquarters
of the Student Non-violent Coordinating Committee (SNCC),
Students for a Democratic Society (SDS), the Dubois Clubs, and
other "Communist dominated, Communist influenced, and Com-

munist oriented" student groups; the third a procession of three ducks with this legend below it: "If it walks like a duck, talks like a duck, and lays eggs like a duck, then it's a duck."

After the showing the commandant requests that the cadets prepare files on fellow-students involved in these organizations. Three trusted Rot-cees are assigned to correlate the information. When the story of this educational operation broke last year, Washington's president sent an outraged letter to the Commanding General of the U.S. Sixth Army. The Army confirmed the report that it was furnishing this "guidance program" material to the ROTC and volunteered the information that the program was being offered in ROTC units at twenty-six colleges in eight Western states.

Three-fourths of the Berkeley student body had voted against compulsory ROTC in 1940; the California regents, pushed by Chancellor Clark Kerr, abolished it in 1962, twenty-two years later. Down the years the Berkeley anti-Rot-cee campaign mounted, and in 1960 a student group announced that it was going to picket. "If I or any of my staff find anyone picketing in uniform," said the campus commandant, "that student may find it very difficult to pass the course." An honor student who had got an A in Rot-cee at mid-term found it not difficult, but impossible. When the National Student Association and other organizations protested that F that followed, the Commandant said that the offender ought to have been expelled and arrested, and the NSA was informed by the Executive Office of the Army Reserve and ROTC Affairs that the action was appropriate reprisal for advocacy of a voluntary program.

Such modest restraint as the "academic" manuals display is not likely to weigh heavily against the officers' lectures, orders, warnings, "guidance kits," and slide shows. The restraint of the ROTC manuals themselves is minimal. Their assumptions are neither arcane nor exotic. The first is that the blessings of life and liberty are won and preserved by war and preparation for war; and the history of the United States is adduced to prove the point. The second is that "world Communism" is the implacable and insatiable enemy of mankind represented by the United States ("and our allies," presently unspecified); that there might be any other enemy or, indeed, any other evil abroad or at home is excluded. The third is that human wickedness (from which the Free World is happily exempt) is the cause of Communism; and the best that can be said for those who think otherwise is that they are "a motley of blind idealists, political opportunists, regenerate [sic] criminals, and misled individuals."

Given the military status of the cadet, the military status of the teacher, and the authority of the U.S. Government as the publisher of the "academic" texts, these two to four years of incessant thunder on the right ought to have a fair chance of transforming (or forming) the susceptible young man into a reflexive defender of a world that never was.

Unless he is a history major, he will never know why, or what, Nazism and Fascism were or, indeed, that there ever were such things; much less, that soldiers were hanged at Nuremberg *because* they obeyed their superior officers' orders. None of these things will he know after reading *The Role of the United States in World Affairs*; or why the free election in Vietnam required by the Geneva Agreement was never held, or how the government of Guatemala was overthrown, or what put an end to the U-2 flights over Russia. What he will know, reading *American Military History*, is that President Truman "relieved General MacArthur of command in the Far East in one of the most controversial episodes of the [Korean] conflict," but he will never know why (or even why it was controversial). But he will have read the sixty-eight-page oversized brochure in technicolor, *Your Career as an Army Officer*, with the following words of General MacArthur centered in headline type on Page 1: "Yours is the profession of arms ... the will to win ... the sure knowledge that in war there is no substitute for victory, that if you lose the nation will be destroyed, that the very obsession of your public service must be duty, honor, country." No one will ever tell him (not even, come to think of it, if he is a history major) about faith, hope, love.

But he is not likely to be a history major if he's in Rot-cee.

His heroes will all be American generals like General MacArthur, whether they won, lost, or drew. And he will learn that when they lost or drew it was still a great day for the Americans: "Although Pershing failed to capture Villa, the activities of American troops in Mexico and along the border were not wasted effort.... Many defects in the Military Establishment, especially in the National Guard, were uncovered in time to correct them before the Army was thrown into the cauldron of war in Europe. One other result that can be attributed to the experiences of the Army on the border, in part at least, was the passage of much-needed legislation affecting national defense."

His heroes will not include civilians *or* admirals — not in *Army* ROTC: "Few Americans at the outset [of the war with Spain] had any notion that the limited campaign envisioned in Cuba and Carribean waters would almost immediately be expanded by an aggressive Navy to include operations on the other side of the world;" but fortunately "the American soldier and his immediate superiors took the bungling in high places in stride and demonstrated an aptitude for improvisation equal to the highest traditions of the Army...."

When it comes to developing *leaders*, the Army does not concede that anything surpasses Rot-cee, and "in the process it also develops the kind of junior executive or manager needed in every field of civilian endeavor." Another of its star-spangled plugs, this one entitled, *Where the Leaders Are*, addresses itself to "the young man who wants to be 'where the leaders are' on his college campus and in a military or civilian career after college," and it warns him that "many college men, if they do not take ROTC, miss this instruction in developing self-discipline, physical stamina, and bearing because comparable leadership training and experience are not normally provided in the academic courses required for a college degree.... No course outside of the ROTC offers this kind of leadership training."

ROTC*

Major William F. Muhlenfeld

Major William F. Muhlenfeld is a career officer in the United States Army Artillery. He was commissioned from the ROTC of Western Maryland College in Westminster, and since returning from Vietnam in January 1967, he has been an instructor with the Army ROTC at Rutgers University.

On a cold, blustery Monday morning in early November 1967, members of the department of military science at Rutgers University found their office building surrounded by students from the campus chapter of the Students for a Democratic Society (SDS). The students would not permit the military staff to enter their building, and a spokesman said they intended to stay where they were until ROTC left the Rutgers campus. For three days and nights they stood their ground. To every effort at breaching the cordon they responded, and they made clear that the building could be entered only at the cost of some kind of violence.

Finally, it all ended. The university administration acted in the interests of order. The students were required to desist. Hearings were held, punishments meted out, disciplinary probations imposed. But ROTC had become a celebrated cause. Crowds of hecklers had gathered. National news networks had come with microphones and TV cameras. The campus newspaper had had a field day. Most important, the administration had set up a faculty-student committee to evaluate the ROTC program. From its recommendations and the ensuing faculty debate came certain reforms — too mild to satisfy the protesters, but strong enough to cast doubts about ROTC's future.

A year has passed since the now famous siege. After a furious faculty debate — notable primarily for the latent hostilities and misunderstandings it revealed — the character of ROTC at Rutgers has been altered slightly. The overall credit for par-

---

* Major William F. Muhlenfeld, "ROTC," *Army* (February 1969), p. 21.

ticipation has been reduced by 14 per cent. Procedures for withdrawal have been simplified. Portions of the ROTC curriculum nominally outside the area of military expertise are to be taught by civilian faculty. Academic credit for drill has been abolished. Incoming officers are to be appointed in the same way as are other faculty; that is, in terms of the breadth of their educational backgrounds and professional achievements, and the faculty committee on appointments is to have veto power over nominations. Generally speaking, the department of military science is to function precisely as does any other department of Rutgers College, and to the extent that this may interfere with fulfillment of the military mission, the professor of military science has a delicate problem. He must not, for example, condone an intensive recruiting campaign, as this is presumed to be an incursion upon the student's free choice.

The net effect of these reforms has been to erode — some might say emasculate — ROTC at Rutgers. Cadet activities, which once indirectly offered academic credit because they were part of the drill program, now are wholly extracurricular, since leadership laboratory itself is a zero credit course. The band, rangers, color guard, drill team and other groups can get operating funds from the student activities committee only if they demonstrate autonomy from ROTC. The department itself, bastion of the "military mind" as it is, survives as a kind of leper colony whose inhabitants are presumed to be a collection of saberrattling, missile-taling madmen. The student newspaper fulminates with vitriolic passages at the slightest provocation. And through it all, freshman enrollment has declined steadily: from 491 in 1966, to 242 in 1967, to 170 in 1968. Why?

The answer to this question is a long one indeed. An objective analysis is especially difficult for anyone with strong feelings about the worth of ROTC, its importance to the military services and its consequent importance to the national interests of the United States.

To begin with, it is specious to suppose that opposition to ROTC stems exclusively or even primarily from liberal opposition to the Vietnam war. That opposition might be a catalyst, a kind of fuze to the Molotov cocktail, as it were, but it is hardly the principal cause. The argument is pleasantly seductive because it suggests that when the war goes away so will opposition to ROTC. Unfortunately, it seems more probable that when the war goes away opposition to ROTC may grow, since in the minds of critics the need for military leaders will have declined. ROTC is quietly tolerated by many academics because they pragmatically realize that the national interest demands it. To discern this unhappy truth, one need only ask a cross-section of the silent majority who decline to join the debate.

Next, it is incorrect to suppose that opposition to ROTC is regional. This understandably myopic assessment usually comes from the Northeast, where those in the eye of the storm believe that, since they inhabit the liberal's traditional domain, they are the sole victims of the wild-eyed attacks against "militarism" on the campus. It is a fact, however, that ROTC has taken its knocks rather generally in the last year and a half. At Michigan State, opponents of ROTC infiltrated "spies" into the program. At Tulane, hooded demonstrations fell into ranks with marching Naval ROTC cadets. At the Chicago Circle campus of Illinois University, pickets appeared at an ROTC review. At Stanford, 13 students (six of them girls) enrolled in ROTC deliberately to ridicule the program. At Howard, students "sat in" upon the president to protest compulsory ROTC. At Boston University, students complained about military "propaganda." The Yale *Daily News* led a campaign to abolish credit for ROTC participation. Objections to compulsory ROTC were in part responsible for demonstrations at Tuskegee Institute where students locked the trustees in a campus guest house. These examples are only a few of those significant enough to attract attention to the public press.

Finally, the standard arguments against ROTC — now repeated so often — are not the real arguments.

Argument number one is that military officers are unfit to join a university faculty, since they do not have doctoral degrees and are not by temperament scholars. This does not, however, preclude the appointment of a selected few others to full faculty status, including full professorships, when they similarly lack formal qualification. Nor does it preclude the referral of teaching duties to "teaching assisants" — young men not yet 25 who themselves only recently have been granted a bachelor's degree.

The next argument attacks the "intellectual content" of ROTC courses. Here one makes the nice distinction between "education" and 'training," and between what is basically "intellectual" and what is basically "professional. The implication is that academic credit should be offered for the one and not for the other. Yet the distinction — and its implications concerning academic credit — is apparently inapplicable to courses concerning piano playing, practice teaching, physical education, and the control of weeds.

Another argument, only slightly more sophisticated, holds that it is contrary to the philosophy of higher education to teach the techniques of violence if, in fact, it truly is devoted to enlightenment and reason. Carried to its logical extension, however, holders of this view finally must agree that it is better for the ignorant and brutal to wage war than for the educated and compassionate.

The last major argument deals with the invidious character of "outside influences." Here, in one's mind's eye, he sees himself locked in a bare room while a poisonous black fluid slowly rolls in under the door. The fluid of the metaphor, of course, is the "military mind," with all of its right-wing conservatism, its unfashionable red-white-and-blue patriotism, its loyalty to the Establishment, its propaganda, its simple-minded solutions to complex problems, its threat to scholarly iconoclasm. What is unclear, however, is that the only outside influence sufficiently threatening to provoke reaction is that of the military. Not government generally. Not the foundations. Not business. Just the military. Once one pokes through the vitriolic haze and grasps this kernel of truth, the whole melancholy litany stands revealed for what it is: an elaborate appartus to justify a prejudice against the military and its ways. What, after all, is more antithetical to free and reasoned dissent than the chain of command? Or to the freedom which must characterize creativity and scholarly inquiry than the regimen of a military organization? And what personal conflict is more inevitable than that between those committed to the former and those committed to the latter?

In terms of faculty opposition to ROTC, what we are seeing is this long latent but fundamental cleavage in full flower, goaded into the open by students who are neither as inhibited nor as prudent as their mentors, and who are untroubled by the injustice of it all because they do not perceive it. Some years ago, Morris Janowitz, the prominent sociologist, recognized the academician's peculiar aversion to military matters when, in his preface to *The New Military*, he felt constrained to justify to his peers the object of his scholarship. By implication, many considered the military unworthy of scholarly attention, just as a local minority considers the military unworthy of a place on the campus. Somehow, that minority will have to decide how it can favor university involvement in the great issues of our time while concurrently attempting to expel from its midst those who need its help; how it can be concerned about social institutions generally but not particularly; how it can seek an enlightened military while seeking to deprive the military of its enlightened leadership; how it can favor participatory democracy while participating itself only selectively.

Yet, one realizes that the untapped reservoir of faculty opposition had been quiescent for years and that it could have been catalyzed into activity only by dissident students. It is to the phenomenon of student activism in the 1960s, then, to which we must turn if we are to speculate further upon the extraordinary confluence of two minorities who, for their separate reasons, jointly seek to undermine ROTC. One finds considerably more cause for charity on behalf of students than for their faculties but, here too, there is a substantial measure of error.

All who are close to higher education recognize the advent of a new era. It is not clear whether the change has been gradual or abrupt, but there is no question that today's student is much more sensitive to his society and concerned about its direction. Moreover, the phenomenon is world-wide in scope and therefore beyond, in the causative sense, national manifestations. Student reaction to national policies is a symptom of student activism and not a cause of it. Neither is it clear why the wave of student concern should have occurred in the decade of the 1960s, rather than, let us say, the 1930s. Probably the expansion of higher education, its mass extension across class lines, improved communications, the vexing problems of the 20th century, our more mobile society — all have something to do with it. But for whatever reason, as students probe their environment and see starvation in Appalachia, the despair of the underprivileged and poverty-stricken, the ofttimes futile strivings of the ethnic minorities, the butchery of modern warfare, the predatory machinations of organized crime, it is understandable that they dissent from the status quo. To many sensitive people, the blunt conclusions of the Kerner report on civil disturbances accurately assess America in the 20th century. For them, it has become a rude, ever-growing split, driven toward divisiveness in the final analysis by its own political and social systems, gone plunging toward destruction like a runaway locomotive. For some, arrest of this rush to oblivion — by the violent overthrow of government if necessary — is the crucial objective. Such people comprise the radical student left, the left wing of which is the Students for a Democratic Society.

On the ROTC issue the SDS is, of course, livid. The Army, in its roles of foreign and domestic "enforcer" for the Establishment, protector of "decadent" government, and practitioner of "genocide," lies beyond the pale. Little wonder, then, that the ROTC program should face the spearhead of their attack and that the guilty university administrations, "enslaved by the Wall Street axis," should finish a close second. The SDS parrots the same anti-ROTC arguments solemnly advanced by their collaborators on the faculty, and to a large extent shares their fundamental antipathy to and revulsion toward things military. But the SDS, in ascribing to the military the intention to preserve by force the status quo, injects a new and quite different purpose for opposition. Presumably, if the Army were committed to altering the status quo, if by some wild turn of events it were of use to the SDS, the ROTC might become a very satisfactory institution indeed. This would not help the professors, however, for the military mind is the military mind, and it would still be around to "contaminate" the campus.

What has happened is that two sources of opposition — one largely ideological and the other largely emotional — have fallen into coincidence and interacted. The students could not have survived without faculty support. The faculty would not have come around without student agitation. The concerted opposition of these two minorities has succeeded in driving from ROTC many of the uncommitted and uncertain majority. Instinctively one realizes, however, that this is by no means the whole story. No one is more inclined toward his own self-interest than the adolescent freshman. Anyone who has counseled a freshman knows well that freshman do what they wish to do, what fits their system of values. After years of parental restraint, the atmosphere of college is headily permissive. We can be assured that if, in the mind of the entering freshman, ROTC were not in the first place a questionable option, attacks upon it would be futile. Clearly, ROTC is an option with important pros and cons. Since the freshman enrolls in the program, one must view it through his eyes and adopt his values in order to understand his decisions. If that is possible, if Chief Justice Earl Warren is wrong in his estimate of the generation gap, within these 18-year-old heads we shall find some important answers. The freshmen control the fate of ROTC; occasionally their organized opposition exercises a frail and fleeting balance of power.

Freshmen entertain some rather ambivalent notions about military service. By and large, they are uninterested in it, not because they are unpatriotic but because, vocationally speaking, they are motivated in other directions. They accept their responsibility to serve in the armed forces if called upon to do so, but many are quite unwilling to *guarantee* that they will do so by joining ROTC — and almost all are uncomfortable at being confronted with the decision during their first week at college, at a time when they have barely registered with the Selective Service System.

In addition, freshmen are inveterate dreamers. Until they come rudely to earth at the end of their first semester, nearly all are going to graduate schools, there to become physicians, lawyers, public administrators and captains of industry. Military service therefore remains comfortably beyond the horizon. Much can happen over five or more years and, for the undergraduate years at the very best, the walls of ivy keep the predatory minions of Selective Service locked securely outside. Only two varieties of frosh enroll in ROTC: the comparatively few who genuinely want to get a commission, and the relative many who have decided sooner or later, one way or the other, they would otherwise be drafted.

The number in this latter group has been shrinking as the anti-ROTC campaign has developed. Because they wish to defer the inevitable decision about military service, they are prey for dissuaders who argue that joining the ROTC is neither necessary nor desirable, and who portray the ROTC cadet as a square and a jerk. That image is not, of course, fully credible; but it is somewhat credible, given the freshman's adolescent values. When it is seen as additive to other factors which in his mind are important, it assumes its significance. Those other factors have been part of ROTC for some time and are a commentary on the Army's failure to move with the times. Some are truly significant and some are not, but all are important since it is not what is real, but what students perceive to be real, that is important.

First among these is drill — what is euphemistically termed "leadership laboratory." It is very hard to find anything good about this anachronism. Surely it cannot be required: ROTC cadets methodically plod through the same close-order rituals each week for four years, in order to master what basic trainees are taught in the first days of their service. Yet, drill has survived for nearly 50 years as the most immutable aspect of ROTC. All the while it has become progressively less relevant and more annoying. Today, since ROTC instructors have exhausted the even remotely conceivable justifications for it, they usually merely dismiss it as undersirable but necessary. This demonstrates to friend and foe alike that the military is in fact unprogressive, inflexible and dogmatic. Moreover, to the cadet it is extremely boring, demeaning because it is mindless and embarassing because it is public. And if that weren't enough, because drill entails the inconvenience of shining brass and shoes, drawing a rifle, putting on a uniform and taking it off, traveling to and from a parade ground, it requires a good deal of time— usually the better part of an afternoon, which sometimes results in schedule conflicts or lateness to other classes. In sum, "leadership laboratory" may well be the programs worst enemy.

The second factor is the uniform. Many cadets apparently do not like to wear their uniforms, and for those of us who have chosen military careers this is difficult to understand. But it is true. One need only observe that, without exception, cadets change clothes at the end of ROTC class whenever they can do so. The cadets give a variety of reasons for this. They say their uniforms fit poorly and are out of style; in particular, some basic course cadets abhor the green garrison cap, which somehow they compare to a freshman beanie. They say the uniforms are uncomfortable and complicated when compared, for example to the leisurely ease of a simple coat an tie. But the most important reason is that the uniform attracts attention. College students, moving through the self-conscious transition to adulthood, do not wish to be the focus of attention. What they wish more than anything is a position of esteem in the body collegiate, to fit in the warp and woof of the collegiate ethos, to mirror the easy sophistication perceived as the mark of the educated man. At the present time, Army green simply is not part of this image.

The third factor is ROTC instruction itself. It is apparently true that ROTC classes do not enjoy high marks in terms of either interest or relevance. Instructors, by and large, do not — and cannot — bring to the classroom the kind of scholarship which is the norm among their civilian colleagues. The Army provides every conceivable instructional aid, many of which are expensive and elaborate, but that cannot overcome the fundamental contrast. The cadets, after all, judge ROTC instruction in terms of the university environment, because that is *their* environment. The course work is entirely new to them; it involves material with which they ofttimes do not relate. The well-greased class, replete with viewgraph projector and working models — the kind that wins approval in the military service schools — probably contributes to the estrangement. To many students, ROTC classes have about them an unreal, mechanical feature which mitigates against the rapport between instructor and student so vital to the educational process. In all events, these are the criticisms that lend credence to unconscionable attacks upon the fundamental worth of the instruction and support the related attempts to remove or reduce academic credit. They are also criticisms that have been voiced for a long time on the campus and today constitute a kind of folklore which freshmen quickly assimilate.

It is no wonder, really, that the axis welded together among faculty and students by the SDS is having an apparent effect. The program has some real faults in the student mind, and it is surprising that these in themselves have not provoked a deleterious effect much sooner and of their own accord. The demands and opportunities in higher education are steadily expanding. Each year more and more interests compete for the student's attention. University life is becoming more dynamic and exciting, for the activism is pervasive. Unless the Army can draw apace of this trend and join it, there will be no hope to infuse ROTC with new vitality. Policy people throughout the Army realize that ROTC must succeed, for the "Reserve" part of "Reserve Officers' Training Corps" has become a misnomer in the last 20 years. The Army depends upon the university to provide the bulk of its commissioned leaders. One need only observe that if West Point were to graduate 1,000 officers a year for 30 years and not one of them resigned, that figure would constitute 20 per cent of a 150,000-man officer corps.

The Army has begun to react. The process of reform has begun, but so far the progress has been slow and unsure. It is undoubtedly true that at the policy level, traditionalists and revisionists have collided over the choice of options. And it is clearly true that soldiers in academia cannot move with celerity and self-confidence as they do on the battlefield. This necessitates some time-consuming poking around to "get the feel of the problem." The ungoldly tedium of the bureaucracy, the staffing process, practical questions of money and resources, the necessity for pilot projects—all these contribute to further delays. It may well be that the element of urgency has also been absent, since declining freshman enrollments do not affect officer production for at least four years. Nonetheless, the four-year Army ROTC program that began in 1919 and remained fundamentally unchanged for 45 years now exhibits some new wrinkles. These date largely from the Revitalization Act of 1964 and generally predate the current ROTC controversy. They also present a new set of conceptual inconsistencies and operational problems. But they are change . . .

The general restructuring of ROTC that appears on the horizon offers an important opportunity to affirm some necessary fundamentals concerning *any* ROTC program.

First, what is most important about ROTC instruction is that it provide a vehicle for evaluating cadets in terms of their commission potential. This is a highly subjective decision which depends for its accuracy on the judgment of commissioned officers. Stated in another way, it is far more important to assure that commissions go to the best potential leaders. Not necessarily the best scholars or the best athletes. Not necessarily any other sort of student. Since this is true, any "new look" must preserve the evaluation opportunity. It must not weaken that opportunity by seriously curtailing the contact between military instructor and cadet, by reducing the number of semesters during which the evaluation is made, or by transferring part of the evaluation responsibility to civilian faculty (who demonstrate by their behavior that they have a poor appreciation of the special demands of officership). One of the weaknesses of the two-year program is that it introduces to the advanced course students of whom the PMS has no prior knowledge while halving his opportunity to evaluate their fitness for commissioned service.

Next, ROTC, because of the way it is structured, must not conflict with other student interests. For example, it must not conflict with the graduation requirements of the institution because it causes scheduling conflicts, academic overloads, credit imbalances which are difficult to adjust, or difficulties with the sequential alignment of courses in the student's major field. ROTC must be *convenient*—and this also again evokes the complaints about leadership laboratory, uniform regulations and other trappings of the military which the cadets don't understand and continually object to. The professor of military science clearly needs a great deal of autonomy in this area, since conditions at institutions vary greatly.

Third, ROTC must be worthwhile in terms of student perceptions just as clearly as commissioned service is worthwhile in terms of officer perceptions. Since only a few students perceive officership in a mature and balanced way, since during college years they themselves are grappling with private identity crises, since it is fundamentally impossible for freshmen to feel strongly about a matter with which they cannot relate, the incentives must be immediate, practical and sufficiently compelling to override doubts. In other words, the incentives must be an end in themselves while the students are learning the meaning of their purpose. Clearly, fear of the draft is the worst sort of incentive. It is unattractive, suggests that an Army commission is the best of poor alternatives, breeds cynicism about the military and its purposes, and therefore attracts many of the wrong people. In the area of attractive incentives, there are a number of possibilities—including substantially higher pay, pay to freshmen, and extension of at least some active duty privileges (such as space-available travel). Such ideas at the very least require major policy decisions because of their cost and implications about membership in the Army Reserve, but they are worth considering.

Finally, ROTC must be supported by institutional administrations and faculty. If, after curriculum reform, efforts to send officers with advanced degrees, and every conceivable accommodation in the area of scheduling, the hostility of an implacable and persistent minority continues to impede the ROTC at every turn while administrators maintain an Olympian silence, the incentives will be strong indeed if they alone are to sustain a healthy program. A principal value of academic credit is that it serves as tangible testimony of the program's worth in the eyes of an institution, and it is that stamp of approval which must pervade the spirit of the relationship as well as it letter. Even though it is true that academic credit has surprisingly little connection with ROTC enrollment, it is equally true that a program without it is likely to subsist on the fringe of the academic community, held in contempt by some, ignored by many, and with small voice in the institutional affairs which are its legitimate concern. This is an ignominious situation which places the Army in the position of groveling for officers, an unworthy role which it ought not countenance.

There is a sad ambiguity about the ROTC controversy. In terms of dissident sentiment the ambiguity is a paradox. Only the naive seriously argue that armies can be eliminated from this unsettled world. But who would not wish it so? In the unhappy interim, while free nations secure themselves with the materials of war, it is of utmost importance that their armies be led by just and compassionate men—men who understand that as leaders they are also public servants who have a profound responsibility to minister to the welfare of those they command, to serve with fidelity, integrity and the wisdom to see beyond their actions to the effects their actions wreak. This kind of leadership must come from the university, where the fundamental humanism undergirding the very concepts of a liberal education thrive and infect those who come to learn. It can come from nowhere else because there is nowhere else. The Army has only a minor influence on the university. The influence of the university on the Army is very great, and its importance is urgent. Among the contributions of the universities to the professions, few are more important than this. The paradox is that we must wait for the professors to learn.

The Military-Industrial-Academic Complex*

William F. Fulbright

While young dissenters plead for resurrection of the American promise, their elders continue to subvert it. As if it were something to be very proud of, it was announced not long ago that the war in Vietnam had created a million new jobs in the United States. Our country is becoming conditioned to permanent conflict. More and more our economy, our Government, and our universities are adapting themselves to the requirements of continuing war—total war, limited war, and cold war. The struggle against militarism into which we were drawn 26 years ago has become permanent, and for the sake of conducting it, we are making ourselves into a militarized society.

I do not think the military-industrial complex is the conspiratorial invention of a band of "merchants of death." One almost wishes that it were, because conspiracies can be exposed and dealt with. But the components of the new American militarism are too diverse, independent, and complex for it to be the product of a centrally directed conspiracy. It is rather the inevitable result of the creation of a huge, permanent military establishment, whose needs have given rise to a vast private defense industry tied to the Armed Forces by a natural bond of common interest. As the largest producer of goods and services in the United States, the industries and businesses that fill military orders will in the coming fiscal year pour some $45 billion into over 5,000 cities and towns where over 8 million

---

* From William F. Fulbright, "The War and Its Effects." Speech before the United States Senate (December 1967).

Americans, counting members of the Armed Forces, comprising approximately 10 percent of the labor force, will earn their living from defense spending. Together all these industries and employees, drawing their income from the $75 billion defense budget, form a giant concentration of socialism in our otherwise free enterprise economy.

Unplanned though it was, this complex has become a major political force. It is the result rather than the cause of American military involvements around the world; but, composed as it is of a vast number of citizens—not tycoons or "merchants of death" but ordinary, good American citizens—whose livelihood depends on defense production, the military industrial complex has become an indirect force for the perpetuation of our global military commitments. This is not—and I emphasize "not"— because anyone favors war but because every one of us has a natural and proper desire to preserve the sources of his livelihood. For the defense worker this means preserving or obtaining some local factory or installation and obtaining new defense orders; for the labor union leader it means jobs for his members at abnormally high wages; for the politician it means preserving the good will of his constituents by helping them to get what they want. Every time a new program, such as Mr. McNamara's $5 billion "thin" antiballistic missile system, is introduced, a powerful new constituency is created—a constituency that will strive mightily to protect the new program and, in the case of the ABM, turn the "thin" system into a "thick" one, movement already underway according to reports in the press. The constituency-building process is further advanced by the perspicacity of Defense officials and contractors in locating installations and plants in the districts of influential key Members of Congress.

In this natural way generals, industrialists, businessmen, labor leaders, workers, and politicians have joined together in a military-industrial complex—a complex which, for all the inadvertency of its creation and the innocent intentions of its participants, has nonetheless become a powerful new force for the perpetuation of foreign military commitments, for the introduction and expansion of expensive weapons systems, and, as a result, for the militarization of large segments of our national life. Most interest groups are counterbalanced by other interest groups, but the defense complex is so much larger than any other that there is no effective counterweight to it except concern as to its impact on the part of some of our citizens and a few of our leaders, none of whom have material incentive to offer.

The universities might have formed an effective counterweight to the military-industrial complex by strengthening their emphasis on the traditional values of our democracy, but many of our leading universities have instead joined the monolith, adding greatly to its power and influence. Disappointing though it is, the adherence of the professors is not greatly surprising. No less than businessmen, workers, and politicians, professors like money and influence. Having traditionally been deprived of both, they have welcomed the contracts and consultantships offered by the Military Establishment.

The great majority of American professors are still teaching students and engaging in scholarly research, but some of the most famous of our academicians have set such activities aside in order to serve their government, especially those parts of the government which are primarily concerned with war.

The bonds between the Government and the universities are no more the results of a conspiracy than those between Government and business. They are an arrangement of convenience, providing the Government with politically usable knowledge and the universities with badly needed funds. Most of these funds go to large institutions which need them less than some smaller and less well-known ones, but they do on the whole make a contribution to higher learning, a contribution, however, which is purchased at a high price.

That price is the surrender of independence, the neglect of teaching, and the distortion of scholarship. A university which has become accustomed to the inflow of government contract funds is likely to emphasize activities which will attract those funds. These, unfortunately, do not include teaching undergraduates and the kind of scholarship which, though it may contribute to the sum of human knowledge and to man's understanding of himself, is not salable to the Defense Department or the CIA. As Clark Kerr, former president of the University of California, expressed it:

The real problem is not one of Federal control but of Federal influence. A Federal agency offers a project. The university need not accept, but as a practical matter, it usually does. . . . Out of this reality have followed many of the consequences of Federal aid for the universities; and they have been substantial. That they are subtle, slowly cumulative and gentlemanly makes them all the more potent.[1]

From what one hears the process of acquiring Government contracts is not always passive and gentlemanly.

One of the dismal sights in American higher education—

Writes Robert M. Rosenzweig, associate dean of the Stanford University graduate division—

is that of administrators scrambling for contracts for work which does not emerge from the research or teaching interests of their faculty. The result of this unseemly enterprise is bound to be a faculty coerced or seduced into secondary lines of interest, or a frantic effort to secure nonfaculty personnel to meet the contractual obligations. Among the most puzzling aspects of such arrangements is the fact that Government agencies have permitted and even encouraged them. Not only are they harmful to the universities—which is not, of course, the Government's prime concern—but they insure that the Government will not get what it is presumably buying; namely, the intellectual and technical resources of the academic community. It is simply a bad bargain all the way around.[2]

Commenting on these tendencies, a special report on government, the universities and international affairs, prepared for the U.S. Advisory Commission on International Educational and Cultural Affairs, points out that—

The eagerness of university administrations to undertake stylized, Government-financed projects has caused a decline in self-generated commitments to scholarly pursuits, has produced baneful effects on the academic mission of our universities, and has, in addition, brought forward some bitter complaints from the disappointed clients.[3]

---

1. Clark Kerr, *The Uses of the University*, (Cambridge: Harvard University Press, 1964), pp. 57-58.
2. Quoted in: Walter Adams and Adrian Jaffe, *Government, The Universities, and International Affairs: A Crisis in Identity*, Special Report Prepared for the U.S. Advisory Commission on International Educational and Cultural Affairs, 90th Congress, 1st Session, House Document No. 120 (Washington: U.S. Government Printing Office, 1967). pp. 5-6.
3. *Ibid.*, p. 6

Among the baneful effects of the Government-university contract system the most damaging and corrupting are the neglect of the university's most important purpose, which is the education of its students, and the taking into the Government camp of scholars, especially those in the social sciences, who ought to be acting as responsible and independent critics of their Government's policies. The corrupting process is a subtle one: no one needs to censor, threaten, or give orders to contract scholars; without a word of warning or advice being uttered, it is simply understood that lucrative contracts are awarded not to those who question their Government's policies but to those who provide the Government with the tools and techniques it desires. The effect, in the words of the report to the Advisory Commission on International Education, is—

To suggest the possibility to a world—never adverse to prejudice—that academic honesty is no less marketable than a box of detergent on the grocery shelf.[4]

The formation of a military-industrial complex, for all its baneful consequences, is the result of great numbers of people engaging in more or less normal commercial activities. The adherence of the universities, though no more the result of a plan or conspiracy, nonetheless involves something else: the neglect and, if carried far enough the betrayal, of the university's fundamental reason for existence, which is the advancement of man's search for truth and happiness. It is for this purpose, and this purpose alone, that universities receive—and should receive—the community's support in the form of grants, loans and tax exemptions.

When the university turns away from its central purpose and makes itself an appendage to the Government, concerning itself with techniques rather than purposes, with expedients rather than ideals, dispensing conventional orthodoxy rather than new ideas, it is not only failing to meet its responsibilities to its students; it is betraying a public trust.

This betrayal is most keenly felt by the students, partly because it is they who are being denied the services of those who ought to be their teachers, they to whom knowledge is being dispensed wholesale in cavernous lecture halls, they who must

---

4. *Ibid.*, p. 8.

wait weeks for brief audiences with important professors whose time is taken up by travel and research connected with Government contracts. For all these reasons the students feel themselves betrayed, but it is doubtful that any of these is the basic cause of the angry rebellions which have broken out on so many campuses.

It seems more likely that the basic cause of the great trouble in our universities is the student's discovery of corruption in the one place, besides perhaps the churches, which might have been supposed to be immune from the corruptions of our age. Having seen their country's traditional values degraded in the effort to attribute moral purpose to an immoral war, having seen their country's leaders caught in inconsistencies which are politely referred to as a "credibility gap," they now see their universities—the last citadels of moral and intellectual integrity —lending themselves to ulterior and expedient ends, and betraying their own fundamental purpose, which, in James Bryce's words, is to "reflect the spirit of the times without yielding to it."

2. Poverty In America

Students are not the only angry people in America, nor the only people with cause for anger. There is also the anger of the American poor, black and white, rural and urban. These are the dispossessed and neglected children of the affluent society, the 32 million Americans whose hopes were briefly raised by the proclamation of a war on poverty, only to be sacrified to the supervening requirements of the war on Asian communism, or, more exactly, to the executive preoccupation and congressional parsimony induced by that war.

In our preoccupation with foreign wars and crises we have scarcely noticed the revolution wrought by undirected change here at home. Since World War II our population has grown by 59 million; a mass migration from country to city has crowded over 70 percent of our population onto scarcely more than 1 percent of our land; vast numbers of rural Negroes from the South have filled the slums of northern cities while affluent white families have fled to shapeless new suburbs, leaving the cities physically deteriorating and financially destitute, and creating a new and socially destructive form of racial isolation combined with degrading poverty. Poverty, which is a tragedy in a poor country, blights our affluent society with something more than tragedy; being unnecessary, it is deeply immoral as well.

Distinct though it is in cause and character, the Negro rebellion is also part of the broader crisis of American poverty, and it is unlikely that social justice for Negroes can be won except as part of a broad program of education, housing and employment for all of our poor, for all of the great "underclass" of whom Negroes comprise no more than one-fourth or one-third. It is essential that the problem of poverty be dealt with as a whole, not only because the material needs of the white and colored poor are the same—better schools, better homes and better job opportunities—but because alleviating poverty in general is also the best way to alleviate racial hostility.

It is not the affluent and educated who account for the "backlash" but the poorer white people, who perceive in the Negro rights movement a threat to their jobs and homes and— probably more important—a threat to their own meager sense of social status.

There is nothing edifying about poverty. It is morally as well as physically degrading. It does not make men brothers. It sets them against each other in competition for jobs and homes and status. It leaves its mark on man and its mark is not pretty. Poverty constricts and distorts, condemning its victims to an endless, anxious struggle for physical necessities. That struggle in turn robs a man of his distinctly human capacities—the capacity to think and create, the capacity to seek and savor the meaning of things, the capacity to feel sympathy and friendliness for his fellow man.

If we are to overcome poverty and its evil byproducts, we shall have to deal with them as human rather than as racial or regional problems. For practical as well as moral reasons, we shall have to have compassion for those who are a little above the bottom as well as for those who are at the bottom. We shall have to have some understanding of the white tenant farmer as well as the Negro farm laborer, of the urban white immigrant workingman as well as the Negro slum dweller. It would even benefit us to acquire some understanding—not approval, just understanding—of each other's group and regional prejudices.

If the racial crisis of recent years has proven anything, it is that none of us, Northerner or Southerner, has much to be proud of, that our failures have been national failures, that our problems are problems of a whole society, and so, as well, must be their solutions.

All these problems—of poverty and race, jobs and schools—have come to focus in the great cities, which, physically, mentally, and esthetically, are rapidly becoming unfit for human habitation. As now taking shape, the cities and suburbs are the product of technology run rampant, without effective political direction, without regard to social and long-term economic cost. They have been given their appearance by private developers, builders and entrepreneurs, seeking, as they will, their own short-term profit.

Rivers and bays are polluted and the air is filled with the fumes of the millions of cars which choke the roads. Recreation facilities and places of green and quiet are pitifully inadequate and there is no escape from crowds and noise, both of which are damaging to mental health.

At the heart of the problem is the absence of sufficient funds and political authority strong enough to control the anarchy of private interest and to act for the benefit of the community. Despite the efforts of some dedicated mayors and students of urban problems, the tide of deterioration is not being withstood and the cities are sliding deeper into disorganization and demoralization.

The larger cities have grown beyond human scale and organizing capacity. No matter what is done to rehabilitate New York and Chicago, they will never be places of green and quiet and serenity, nor is there much chance that these can even be made tolerably accessible to the millions who spend their lives enclosed in concrete and steel. Ugly and inhuman though they are, the great urban complexes remain nonetheless a magnet for Negroes from the South and whites from Appalachia. Crowding the fetid slums and taxing public services, they come in search of jobs and opportunity, only to find that the jobs which are available require skills which they lack and have little prospect of acquiring.

One wonders whether this urban migration is irreversible, whether it may not be possible to create economic opportunities in the small towns and cities where there are space and land

and fresh air, where building costs are moderate and people can still live in some harmony with natural surroundings. The technology of modern agriculture may inevitably continue to reduce farm employment, but we have scarcely begun to consider the possibilities of industrial decentralization—of subsidies, tax incentives and other means—to make it possible for people to earn a living in the still human environments of small town America.

A decent life in a small town is not only very much better than slum life in a big city; it is probably cheaper too. The Secretary of Agriculture has suggested that it would be better to subsidize a rural family with $1,000 a year for 20 years than to house them in a cramped urban "dwelling unit" at a cost of $20,000. In New York or Chicago $2,500 a year of welfare money will sustain a family in destitution; in the beautiful Ozark country of Arkansas it is enough for a decent life.

Aggravating the material ills is the impersonalization of life in a crowded, urban America. Increasingly we find wherever we go—in shops and banks and the places where we work—that our names and addresses no longer identify us; the IBM machines require numbers—ZIP codes, account numbers, and order numbers. Our relevant identity in a computerized economy is statistical rather than personal. Business machines provide standard information and standard services and there are no people to provide particular information or services for our particular needs.

The governing concept, invented I believe in the Pentagon, is "cost effectiveness," which refers not to the relationship of cost to human need or satisfaction but to the relationship of cost to the computerized system. Technology has ceased to be an instrument of human ends; it has become an end in itself, unregulated by political or philosophical purpose. The toll which all this takes on the human mind can only be guessed at, but it must surely be enormous, because human needs are different from the needs of the system to which they are being subordinated. Someday the human requirements may be computerized too, but they have not, thank God, been computerized yet.

The cost of rehabilitating America will be enormous, beyond anything we have even been willing to think about. When Mayor

Lindsay said that it would cost $50 billion over 10 years to make New York a fit place to live in, his statement was dismissed as fanciful, although $50 billion is less than we spend in 2 years in Vietnam. The Swedish sociologist Gunnar Myrdal has ventured the guess that it will cost trillions of dollars to rehabilitate our slums and their inhabitants.

[T]he common idea that America is an immensely rich and affluent country—

He says—

is very much an exaggeration. American affluence is heavily mortgaged. America carries a tremendous burden of debt to its poor people. That this debt must be paid is not only a wish of the do-gooders. Not paying it implies the risk for the social order and for democracy as we have known it.[5]

Before we can even begin to think of what needs to be done and how to do it, we have got to reevaluate our national priorities. We have got to weigh the costs and benefits of going to the moon against the costs and benefits of rehabilitating our cities. We have got to weigh the costs and benefits of the supersonic transport, which will propel a few business executives and Government officials across the Atlantic in 2 or 3 hours, against the costs and benefits of slum clearance and school construction, which would create opportunity for millions of our deprived "underclass."

We have got to weigh the benefits and consider the awesome disparity of the $904 billion we have spent on military power since World War II as against the $96 billion we have spent, out of our regular national budget, on education, health, welfare, housing, and community development.

Defining our priorities is more a matter of moral accounting than of cost accounting. The latter may help us determine what we are able to pay for, but it cannot help us to decide what we want and what we need and what we are willing to pay for. It cannot help the five-sixths of us who are affluent to decide

5. Gunnar Myrdal, "The Necessity and Difficulty of Planning the Future Society," Address to the National Consultation on the Future Environment of a Democracy: The Next Fifty Years, 1967-2017, called by the American Institute of Planners, Washington, D.C., October 3, 1967, p. 15.

whether we are willing to pay for programs which will create opportunity for the one-sixth who are poor; that is a matter of moral accounting.

It cannot help us to decide whether beating the Russians to the moon is more important to us than purifying our poisoned air and lakes and rivers; that, too, is a matter of moral accounting. Nor can it help us to decide whether we want to be the arbiter of the world's conflicts, the proud enforcer of a pax Americana, even though that must mean the abandonment of the Founding Fathers' idea of America as an exemplary society, and the betrayal of the idea of world peace under world law, which, as embodied in the Covenant of the League of Nations and the Charter of the United Nations, was also an American idea. These, too, are matters of moral accounting.

The American Example

Rich and powerful though our country is, it is not rich or powerful enough to shape the course of world history in a constructive or desired direction solely by the impact of its power and policy. Inevitably and demonstrably, our major impact on the world is not in what we do but in what we are. For all their worldwide influence, our aid and our diplomacy are only the shadow of America; the real America—and the real American influence—are something else They are the way our people live, our tastes and games, our products and preferences, the way we treat each other, the way we govern ourselves, the ideas about man and man's relations with other men that took root and flowered in the American soil.

History testifies to this. A hundred years ago England was dominant in the world, just as America is today. Now England is no longer dominant; her great fleets have vanished from the seas and only fragments remain of the mighty British Empire. What survives? The legacy of hatred survives—hatred of the West and its arrogant imperialism, hatred of the condescension and the exploitation, hatred of the betrayal aboard of the democracy that Englishmen practiced at home. And the ideas survive—the ideas of liberty and tolerance and fair play to which Englishmen were giving meaning and reality at home while acting on different principles in the Empire. In retrospect, it seems clear that England's lasting and constructive impact on modern India, for example, springs not from the way she ruled in India but, despite that, from the way she was ruling England at the same time.

Possessed as they are of a genuine philanthropic impulse, many Americans feel that it would be selfish and exclusive, elitist and isolationist, to deny the world the potential benefits of our great wealth and power, and to restrict ourselves to a largely exemplary role.

It is true that our wealth and power can be, and sometimes are, beneficial to foreign nations, but they can also be, and often are, immensely damaging and disruptive. Experience—ours and that of others—strongly suggests that the disruptive impact predominates, that, when big nations act upon small nations, they tend to do them more harm than good. This is not necessarily for lack of good intentions; it is rather for lack of knowledge. Most men simply do not know what is best for other men, and when they pretend to know or genuinely try to find out, they usually end up taking what they believe to be best for themselves as that which is best for others.

Conceding this regrettable trait for human nature, we practice democracy among ourselves, restricting the freedom of individuals to impose their wills upon other individuals, restricting the state as well, and channeling such coercion as is socially necessary through community institutions. We do not restrict the scope of Government because we wish to deny individuals the benefits of its wealth and power; we restrict our Government because we wish to protect individuals from its capacity for tyranny.

If it is wisdom to restrict the power of men over men within our society, is it not wisdom to do the same in our foreign relations? If we cannot count on the benevolence of an all-powerful Government toward its own people, whose needs and characteristics it knows something about and toward whom it is surely well disposed, how can we count on the benevolence of an all-powerful America toward peoples of whom we know very little? Clearly, we cannot, and, until such time as we are willing to offer our help through community institution such as the

United Nations and the World Bank, I think that, in limiting our commitments to small nations, we are doing more to spare them disruption than we are to deny them benefits.

Mr. President, I might add that it has struck me as rather inconsistent that some of my friends who are most devoted to the rights of the States in domestic affairs are, at the same time, very determined to project our Nation's power into the affairs of peoples abroad.

Wisdom consists as much in knowing what you cannot do as in knowing what you can do. If we knew and were able to acknowledge the limits of our own capacity, we would be likely, more often than we do, to let nature take its course in one place and another, not because it is sure or even likely to take a good course but because, whatever nature's course may be, tampering with it in ignorance will almost surely make it worse.

We used, in the old days, to have this kind of wisdom and we also knew, almost instinctively, that what we made of ourselves and of our own society was far more likely to have a lasting and beneficial impact on the world than anything we might do in our foreign relations. We were content, as they say, to let conduct serve as an unspoken sermon. We knew that it was the freedom and seemingly unlimited opportunity, the energy and marvelous creativity of our diverse population, rather than the romantic nonsense of "manifest destiny," that made the name of America a symbol of hope to people all over the world.

We knew these things until events beyond our control carried us irrevocably into the world and its fearful problems. We recognized thereupon, as we had to, that some of our traditional ideas would no longer serve us, that we could no longer, for example, regard our power as something outside of the scales of the world balance of power, and that, therefore, we could no longer remain neutral from the major conflicts of the major nations.

But, as so often happens when ideas are being revised, we threw out some valid ideas with the obsolete ones. Recognizing that we could not help but be involved in many of the world's crises, we came to suppose that we had to be involved in every crisis that came along; and so we began to lose the understanding of our own limitations.

Recognizing that we could not help but maintain an active foreign policy, we came to suppose that whatever we hoped to accomplish in the world would be accomplished by acts of foreign policy, and, this—as we thought—being true, that foreign policy must without exception be given precedence over domestic needs; and so we began to lose our historical understanding of the power of the American example.

The loss is manifest in Vietnam. There at last we have embraced the ideas that are so alien to our experience—the idea that our wisdom is as great as our power, and the idea that our lasting impact on the world can be determined by the way we fight a war rather than by the way we run our country. These are the principal and most ominous effects of the war—the betrayal of ideas which have served America well, and the great moral crisis which that betrayal has set loose among our people and their leaders.

The crisis will not soon be resolved, nor can its outcome be predicted. It may culminate, as I hope it will, in a reassertion of the traditional values, in a renewed awareness of the creative power of the American example. Or it may culminate in our becoming an empire of the traditional kind, ordained to rule for a time over an empty system of power and then to fade or fall, leaving, like its predecessors, a legacy of dust.

Classified Military Research and the University*

Anatol Rapoport

The university should be a community of scholars dedicated to the pursuit of truth—a hackneyed phrase, perhaps, but a deeply meaningful one to those so dedicated.

---

* Anatol Rapoport, "Classified Military Research and the University," *The Humanist* (January-February 1969), p. 4.

munity. A department store, for example, may be an eminently useful institution, a triumph of marketing techniques, an indis-

Not every socially useful institution can or need be a compensible adjunct to urban society. But a department store is not, and need not be, designed as a community. The only connection between its various services, from selling furniture to duplicating keys, is geographic proximity for the convenience of the shoppers. Neither the shoppers nor the salespeople at different counters need to have anything to do with each other in order for the department store to fulfill its function properly.

I reject the department-store model of the university, the so-called "multiversity," because it is incompatible with the community model; and, I repeat, this does not in any way reflect any judgment on my part as to which of the institutions is the more important to a society. I do have an opinion, but it is not relevant to my argument. It follows that I reject the notion that the university must serve "society" in whatever way society wants to be served as long as such service does not jeopardize other activities essential to the university's mission. The implication of this notion is that such other activities are not jeopardized by the services rendered by the university, as long as the two functions are kept apart. I argue, however, that if different activities in a university have no effect upon one another, then this is prima facie evidence that the university is not a community and therefore its primary function has already been jeopardized.

My objection to conducting classified research in a university is that such activities jeopardize the community a university ought to be and to which members of the university, faculty and students alike, ought to aspire. The community is jeopardized not so much by the distinction between two classes of faculty, those "in" and those "out." After all, every specialist is privy to knowledge inaccessible to those outside his specialty. The university community is jeopardized by secret military research by virtue of the fact that for the most part those who participate in such research owe allegiance to another community, a loyalty that is, in my opinion, incompatible with the loyalty to the community a university ought to be. Moreover, the defense community (or the "strategic community," as it is sometimes called by some of its prominent members) is now a reality, while the

hindrances to the realization of this ideal, but the overlap be-
community of scholars is still only an ideal. There are many
tween the academy and the defense community is, I believe, one
of the most important of these factors.

The intellectual defense community arose in the United
States in the course of the infiltration of military research into
the universities since World War II. The circumstances and
some of the effects of that infiltration are well known. It must
be kept in mind that actual figures tell little of what has happened. Its most important effects have been not quantitative
but qualitative; and they must be considered not only with regard to what is happening to universities but also with regard
to what is happening to the war business. Specifically, not only
has a large sector of the academy become militarized but the
war business has become intellectualized; and because of this
it has become highly attractive to many people who work with
their brains.

It must be borne in mind that dedication to truth as a way
of life is a primary motivating factor to relatively few people.
Most of us have absorbed the cultural values around us as a
matter of course. Among these is an appetite for prestige in
terms of the culturally dominant criteria: being near to the foci
of power, being valued for one's expertise by those who possess
great social prestige, being asked by the wielders of power to
advise on matters of policy, etc. These satisfactions, so long
denied to the American scientist and scholar, coupled with considerable intellectual challenge in the design of military technology and of global diplo-military strategy, were, I am sure, an
important factor in the creation of the scientific-technical defense community. It is a large community ...

But the defense community, it seems to me, is held together
by values quite different and essentially incompatible with the
values that ought to hold together the academic-intellectual
community. I say "ought" because I keep in mind that the latter
is still only an ideal, while the former actually exists. Morever,
it seems to me, the intellectual community is hindered from
maturing by its infusion of academic with the spirit and aims
of the defense community.

The primary value of the would-be intellectual community
is the unfettered search for the truth and its free dissemina-

tion. Closely allied but, at times, only a derivative value is the use of knowledge in the service of humanity. The primary aim of the defense community, on the other hand, is to put power at the disposal of specific groups of men. Since scientific knowledge is a source of power, the defense community seeks such knowledge; and since this knowledge is genuine only if one is aware of truth, the defense community adheres to standards of scientific truth in matters relevant to its pursuits. But in this scheme the awareness of truth is a derivative, not a primary value. In matters not relevant to its pursuits, the defense community is often indifferent to truth. It either takes for granted the world picture of the power wielders or eschews altogether the task of trying to understand the world in which we live. . . .

If the members of the defense community were also true members of the intellectual community, then they would, of course, be completely entitled to defend their world picture. The intellectual community is inherently antidogmatic; and the views of an Edward Teller or a Herman Kahn would be entitled to be heard and discussed side by side with those of a Linus Pauling, a Kenneth Boulding, or an Erich Fromm. But the defense community is not part of the intellectual community. The loyalties of its members are elsewhere, primarily to power, and to truth only in so far as knowing truth helps in the pursuit of power. The work of the defense community does not, in my opinion, help mankind. It is, on the contrary, a threat to mankind. Now this opinion is, naturally, challengeable; but it is also a challenge. The defense community is not obliged to respond to this challenge. Under the cloak of secrecy. . . .

Let us, then, consider a biologist who is doing "basic" research instigated by a felt need in the defense community for more knowledge about pathogenic micro-organisms, knowledge that will facilitate the creation of strains more resistant to antibiotics. The work itself may be of fundamental importance to biology and may be pregnant with "spin-offs." However, the identity of the contracting agency and the secrecy attending the research bespeaks the intended use of this knowledge. Now the "academic freedom" of the scientist to seek such knowledge is not at issue. What is at issue is the fact that, if he does his work in secret, he is not obligated to justify it, if challenged on moral grounds. It is irrelevant whether the example chosen is realistic or not, or what particular parts of war research happen to be done in what specific universities at this time. As long as research is done in secret, we do not know what research is done where, and why. I think a member of a university faculty has a right to know what research is being done under the auspices of his institution; not only the titles of contracts and their sources and budgets but also the content of the research, its applications and implications. I think that the fraud perpetrated by the Central Intelligence Agency on Michigan State University is a blot on that university's name, and I know personally that many faculty members of that university felt a deep shame when the unsavory role of their institution was publicly revealed. . . .

Recall the controversy concerning subversion on campus of a decade and a half ago. There were those who were genuinely devoted to academic freedom and who staunchly defended the Communist's right to his view as a member of a university faculty. They were most concerned, however, with the alleged secrecy of the Communist's activities and commitments. They felt they had a right to know who their colleagues were, not in order to persecute them but in order to be in a position to dissociate themselves from them if their consciences demanded it. An intellectual should have the opportunity to dissociate himself from colleagues who, by serving a war-waging state, violate his moral sense. He should also have the right to dissociate himself from an institution that has become an adjunct of a war-waging state. He cannot do so if research is cloaked in secrecy.

To summarize, the following arguments have been used in defense of classified research on campuses:

(1) Academic freedom has been invoked. The appeal to academic freedom is, in my opinion, irrelevant. If such freedom means anything, it must include the freedom to disseminate knowledge to everyone, not just to privileged groups. The scientist ought to be free to undertake any research that interests him, but he should be in a position to defend his choice to his colleagues. Secrecy cancels this responsibility and is therefore antithetical to academic freedom.

(2) Service rendered to the military establishment has been equated with service rendered to society. I think it is time to turn a jaundiced eye on the proposition that what is good for

the Pentagon is good for the country, or, for that matter, that what is good for this country is necessarily good for man. A university community ought to be an integral part of a world intellectual community and ought to dissociate itself from the power struggles waged by states, blocs of states, and super-states. In this respect, the goals of the intellectual community ought to resemble the goals of a genuinely dedicated religious community, not, of course, in the sense of shared dogmas but in the sense of shared values.

(3) Unclassified "spin-off" from classified research has been cited in the defense of such research. This is no reason for keeping classified research on campus. Spin-offs would presumably occur wherever such research is done. All in all, it is not likely that science would be impoverished if all military research would suddenly stop, let alone if it were excluded from universities.

(4) I will simply dismiss the defense of classified research on the grounds that it brings in money or helps maintain the interest of the military contracting agencies in the research potential of a university. I reject the idea that a university is an enterprise "in the business" of doing research. I have not heard this conception of the university explicitly defended on all campuses, but I must say in all frankness that it is implicit in many of the arguments that I have heard in defense of classified research.

This orientation has also a broader connotation. In the popular mind, the image of a university as a "research business" and an "education business" has become prevalent. Ironically, it is this image that has "legitimatized" the activity of the intellectual in our culture in which the business enterprise is the universal model of all organized activity, all the way from the theater to war. In the business world, growth, solvency, and success in competition are the imperatives of existence. They have been traditionally the dominant values of our society. It has come about, however, that these values are now not only being questioned but actively rejected by a growing sector of our youth; and I am convinced that the ferment on campuses is an expression of a deep resentment on the part of this sector that expects to find other viable values in what ought to be an intellectual community, but instead finds the predominant values of an outlook it has rejected. The *gleichschaltung* of universities to the needs of the business and military world is the most salient symptom of the university's failure to provide a new source of values. Exclusion of classified military research will not, of course, remake the university into a semblance of an intellectual community, but it is an indispensable step in that direction.

(5) Participation in classified research has been cited as a factor in nurturing the scientific interest and the creative interest of the participants. I concede this argument, but at the same time plead for weighing the benefits so derived against the demoralization of other faculty members. The well-known free market principle embodied in the admonition "If you don't like it here, you can go elsewhere" ought to apply more properly to the members of the scientific-technical defense community than to those who view themselves as members of an incipient world intellectual community. The former already have institutions with aims coinciding with their own — the military research institutes specifically created to serve the needs of the military establishment. The latter should also have the right to build their own communities dedicated exclusively to the pursuit of truth, to the dissemination of truth, unencumbered by the needs of the military establishment for secrecy, and to service rendered to all of humanity rather than to groups engaged in a struggle for power.

In Response

Editor's note: Anatol Rapoport's article was sent out for comment to various authors. We are pleased to publish their replies.

Alfred de Grazia:

I cannot find much of a theory in the eminent theorist's diatribe against classified military research, and therefore comment in kind.

I love an open society and I hate secrets. Some of my best friends keep secrets (the scoundrels!). My own life has unfortunately involved many secrets.

I have met men who carry a secret and they are unpleasant men. Some men are power-hungry and, like professors without ideas, gather secrets so as never to be starved out of their strongholds. Then there are all the secrets that are too banal to be publicized; those who hold them are ashamed to reveal them. One could go on; but the point is that most secrets are not worth keeping — or learning. Most classified research is for the birds.

But professors, unlike the birds, try to supplement their incomes. They feel that they need to get equipment, travel, meet people, blow their minds, etc., and classified research helps them do these things. Why keep them from it?

That's the question: Why? Professor Rapoport elevates the question sky-high. He talks of an academic community that doesn't exist and of a defense community that he says (regretfully) exists. He says secrets spoil the academic community. (I think they also usually spoil the defense community.)

But this academic community that we adore — this womb of pure scholarship — where is it? Peel away all the dependencies of classified military and nonmilitary research, and little is left — maybe some Chaucerian scholars (with their cryptic specialties), cuneiform experts (half-a-dozen vestal virgins), and organ-grinders to whom knowledge is a potpourri that they crank out.

I have news for Professor Rapoport. Practically everything is classified. Eighteen years ago I suggested limited outside access to Survey Research Center punched-card files and heard a lot of tongue-clicking. (The situation is now greatly improved.) Yet here is a group as pure as they come. Move to the condition of the pure astronomers and pure physicists and pure psychologists: They're so open-minded that they squirrel away their ideas and will fight you tooth and nail for the right to date their manuscript ahead of yours. Still they love that word "pure," although, or perhaps because, it is devoid of operational meaning.

Then go on to a hundred departments and schools. In all of them professors hold their secrets — the secrets of many types of clients. Following Rapoport's logic, why shouldn't we know who is being interviewed by a teaching psychiatrist or social worker, and why, and whether he is being paid for the knowledge he is concomitantly gaining? Or why shouldn't we bar all corporate, legal, and foundation consultantships, all studies for school boards, all party politicking, all confidential client and subject relations?

Are 2,000 practicing Democratic political scientists going to be made to spill their party secrets to their Republican students? Do we bar medical-school faculty from practicing? No, even though they return to our halls with green on their hands and secrets in their hearts, for we know from the history of science what can happen when medical teaching is kept from bodily contact. And anyway, they won't let us stop them.

In a strangely limited search for a supporting example, Rapoport says we should demand that Communists reveal their secret red selves, so that we can have the pleasure of shunning them. Why not homosexuals, too? Why not the shadowy informants of deans and trustees? Why not everyone? Let us all confess and do it publicly: we of the great Rapoport Academic Community — no secrets, please!

The wicked secret, of course, is the defense secret. "Purge the academic womb of these wickedly secret men, if not of the others." It is not the secret that is disliked; it is the wicked kind of work involved. Never mind that most nonacademic people think classified military research is more noble than the other kinds of classified work. Why not say it? "Let no true academic womb sustain this martial worm." Very well, then there will be no one who will talk intelligently of what went on in the martial community. We would dance around it like savages about a secret source. Whom would this benefit: scientists, students, public, opposing politicians, pacifists? None of these; no one at all. We should become ignorant victims, paranoid dogmatists, smiling organ-grinders.

It occurs to me that, in the "defense" field as any other, a man should do his duty by his academic community; he should translate his private knowledge into public form; he should teach the young and old to think; he should do good research. In short, he should be a good professor and scholar. If he can be so, and wants to, or has to keep secrets, that's his business. It he cannot be a good professor, he should be fired.

Pari passu, a university administration that cannot administer classified projects in ways that are congenial to our academic way of life should not allow them in or should be fired if it does. But why blame classified military research for the massive delinquencies of our universities? It is merely a leaking tap in this slum dwelling. If the reason is to help raze the slum, well then, that is another matter.

Henry M. Pachter:

Terms such as "secret" and "classified" often apply not to the results of research but to the techniques. During the war I was interested in certain violence the Nazis had done to the German language; but to gain access to monitored transcripts of German broadcasts I had to have "clearance." The results of my studies were shared with the "community of scholars," though their ostensible purpose had been "defense." On the other hand, after Hiroshima I wrote to a dozen nuclear physicists imploring them to go on strike and to deny the military any further knowledge of their ghastly invention — but received unanimous refusals on the ground that science could not be stopped. H. L. Nieburg has shown in *In the Name of Science* how the scientists themselves are pushing projects that place them in a commanding position and how they become research tycoons who milk the public treasury under the pretext of "defense." Other examples point in the opposite direction; "Little black boxes" were to record earth tremors and underground explosions; though invented through classified research, their purpose was to police a nuclear-test-halt agreement, a first step towards disarmament.

Classified research is not necessarily connected with warlike purposes and is not necessarily imposed by a scheming "defense community" on a reluctant "community of scholars." The latter simply does not exist; few departments are even on speaking terms with each other; nor do the denizens of one school understand the language and research methods of the other. It is fortunate if some scholars read outside their field; but the average American professor is no philosophe in pure, disinterested pursuit of eternal truth. If he teaches history and political science, he knows that he is training future diplomats, propagandists, and ideologists — at best — and rarely finds among his graduate students one who is interested in theory. Even in the humanities we cannot be sure that our research will not prove beneficial to some commercial or political interests, and there is practically no discovery in the behavioral sciences that has not been used in advertising.

All of this I regret as much as Mr. Rapoport does, but I don't think it is helpful to close our eyes to the obvious fact (the "truth" that Mr. Rapoport claims to pursue) that the university serves the needs and purposes of the community. The question is: Who determines these purposes? Obviously, as long as we have private universities, they will meet the demand of the institutions that finance them. The state universities, on their side, will follow the educational and other goals that have been set by the people's elected representatives, controlled by a free press and open debate. Whether these purposes of the community are humanitarian and praiseworthy (such as social work, urbanism, engineering in the underdeveloped countries) or whether they are dangerous (wasn't LSD invented by academic research?) and in Mr. Rapoport's eyes detestable (defense-connected research) they are all encroachments on the ideal of pure research, and on principle the academy must defend itself against all such demands of the market and of the community.

It does this by imposing conditions on its services: It must be allowed to follow its own methods of research; it must be allowed to train scholars in the spirit of dispassionate, disinterested science; it does not adjust its curriculum to the day-to-day demands of the community but formulates educational goals for the community — and it fights, or should fight with all its might against the ideal of "committed" science. The ethical judgment on the question of whether a particular project of research should be undertaken must be made before the work is assigned. But this decision has many more ramifications than Professor Rapoport seems to realize; he casts a "jaundiced eye" only on military research. Why not on certain kinds of business research, too? Much of this business research, incidentally, requires even more secrecy than military research. Moreover, I remember how sorry the Spanish republicans were that so few of them had studied military science; my eye is only half-jaundiced. Finally, in some recent student rebellions the question was asked whether the scholarly ideal of the pure quest for truth (for instance, whether Shakespeare was the thirteenth Earl of Oxford) was not just a bourgeois device to keep good minds from thinking of revolution.

It seems to me that Professor Rapoport is confusing the issues. One is the morality of certain research, whether academic or otherwise; clearly this must be left to the conscience of those who engage in it, and cannot be the concern of anyone who sets himself up as his brother's keeper. Another question is the academic privilege of setting its own standards of research, of communication, and of recruitment. A third is whether the aims of the academy can be preserved if professors jet around as government consultants and promoters of causes or seek positions in nonacademic bodies. As a citizen, of course, each professor should have the right and the duty to give his knowledge and abilities to any cause he chooses — on his own time, however, and not part of his job. But today business, government, and foundations alienate the professors from their profession. The quest for power is being substituted for the quest for knowledge; they are being called away from their calling. One remedy, of course, would be to seek a strict separation of the academy from purpose-directed projects and service research. Weapons research belongs in army arsenals; professors who accept grants from foundations and other outside agencies should be barred from teaching and publishing. Those who stay in the academy should renounce the advantages in terms of income, secretarial and research help, travel, etc., that have come to them in the last 40 years; they should not write recommendations for their students but educate them in the ideal of purposeless studies. I am prepared to return to the ivory tower but not to a tower of pompous hypocrites who pretend to represent an order that they have long repudiated.

Ernest Van Den Haag:

Professor Rapoport would expel from universities researchers whose work is secret or puts "power at the disposal of specific groups" or is financed by military agencies. They form the "defense community." What, or who, would be excluded? All defense agency funded research whether or not concerned with weapons? Nonsecret military research and secret non-military research? Does either put "power at the disposal of specific groups" more than, i.e., industrial research, leading to patents? Or does Professor Rapoport dislike the "specific group of men" who, he presumes, would get the power more than others? Anyway, does the "defense community" put "power at the disposal" of the President, of generals, of scientists, or of Americans as distinguished from Russians?

Professor Rapoport cannot know which research will ultimately serve peace or war; which research will deter a Stalin or a Mao, defeat a Hitler, or help attack a Castro. The intent of the research (hard to establish anyway) cannot guide us — Professor Rapoport notwithstanding — to the effect. (For example, research on poison gas — regardless of intent — may be useful for (1) protection, if gas is used by others; (2) industrial protection; (3) medical uses.) A case may be made for pure research for "the community of scholars" and against applied science and "social service." But Professor Rapoport only pretends to make this case in order to attack defense research. He ignores schools of business, education, nursing, home economics, physical education, or journalism, none of which do more — at best — than serve society by providing personnel.

The university community is jeopardized, according to Professor Rapoport, because scholars who participate in secret military research "owe allegiance to another community whose loyalty is, in my opinion, incompatible with loyalty to the community the university ought to be." Yet we all owe allegiance to more than one institution or community, i.e., family, church, university, country, party, profession, research institute, project, etc. Our loyalty to such groups may exceed that to the community of scholars (if they were commensurable). This has never been regarded as objectionable. Professor Rapoport's point thus must be that (a) the loyalty to the defense community is incompatible with loyalty to the university community; (b) that this incompatible loyalty to the defense community necessarily, or usually, prevails over loyalty to the university. Both points must be true if the argument is to make sense — yet Professor Rapoport proves neither. Indeed, he makes no serious attempt — other than by asseveration — to show that the members of the defense community are more loyal to it than to the community of scholars — I suspect that the opposite is more often the case

— or to show that the loyalties are in conflict, let alone incompatible. Why is membership in the defense community less compatible with membership in the community of scholars than membership in the Democratic party, the Presbyterian Church, or the Mathematical Association? Why is defense research less compatible with membership in the community of scholars than research in race relations?

According to Professor Rapoport, the university community is devoted to the "search for truth and its free dissemination," and secondarily to "the use of knowledge in the service of man," whereas the defense community is interested primarily in "specific groups of men," and in truth only "in the pursuit of specific knowledge." The incompatibility is factitious. Certainly search for truth or knowledge is what research is about. But it is always specific truth that is sought. How can one see truth in general? Whether truth is the primary aim or prestige, money, or a particular application — such as getting a man to the moon, saving a child, or deterring an enemy — is hard to establish and irrelevant. As for "knowledge in the service of man," both pacifists and militarists believe that their activities are devoted to it. How can one part of the community of scholars decide that another does not serve man?

Professor Rapoport seems to equate "free dissemination" of knowledge with compulsory immediate dissemination. This is an odd usage. Hasn't it always been the privilege of the researcher to disclose or not to disclose his results whenever he chooses? Isn't any scientist morally free not to disclose his nuclear research to a Nazi or Soviet society that, in his opinion, would misuse it, and to disclose it to a democratic one? What else are our military researchers doing? They hand their results to those whom they trust and exclude those whom they don't trust. Ultimately these results will become, *nolente volente*, available to all, as the history of nuclear research indicates. But I see no objection to withholding such results from those who, in the opinion of the researchers, or of the government they trust, may misuse them, or are not entitled to them. (Similar reasoning applies to any, including industrial, research.) There is no *obligation* to disclose research results to colleagues either.

Professor Rapoport also reproaches the defense community with being "indifferent to truth . . . in matters not relevant to its pursuits." Is this more true for defense researchers than for others? Some people are exclusively interested in their specialty and others in matters that go beyond. Professor Rapoport feels that his stricture applies to the defense community specifically, because its members believe that "war research is . . . a 'service to society.' Preparations for war are blithely assumed to increase the nation's 'security.' War itself is justified as regrettable but necessary. . . ." These views Professor Rapoport cannot "otherwise explain" unless "complete dedication to the truth" is not part of "the ethics . . . of the defense community." This assertion tells us more about Professor Rapoport's dogmatism than about the ethics of the defense community. The views he disapproves of are held by many scholars no less ethical, intelligent, or truthful than Professor Rapoport. He wishes to expel the members of the defense community from the community of scholars simply because they do not share his views. Many nonmembers don't either. And few members of either community will share his fanaticism.

Professor Rapoport disguises his intolerance by suggesting that the members of the defense community would be entitled to defend their views if only they "were truly members of the intellectual community," in which case "the views of Edward Teller and Herman Kahn would be entitled to be heard." But the defense community is not part of the intellectual community and therefore is "able to hide behind the cloak of secrecy." Actually Teller and Kahn (and many others) have been quite articulate in defense of their work. The secrecy of some of their work has not hindered rational discussion of its justification. The issue of secrecy thus is quite irrelevant.

Elsewhere Professor Rapoport objects to academicians doing research when their colleagues "do not know what research is done, where and why." Disclosure would enable him "to dissociate himself from colleagues who, by serving a war-waging state, violate his moral sense." I think he is able to do so without detailed disclosure.

Most important, I do not think that membership in a university involves, as Professor Rapoport thinks, "shared values (religious schools excepted)." The "community of scholars" can exist if the members feel that each is entitled to his own values unshared by the others. The members need share only one value, a common dedication to the pursuit of truth, not to its dissemination nor to any other "service to mankind," since this "service" may include sincerely pursued but inconsistent values and policies. The community of scholars has never arrogated the authority (nor does it have criteria) to decide what truly serves mankind. Professor Rapoport mentions that those who defended Communists on campus had qualms about "secrecy." But those who opposed them — as I did and do — did not do so because of "the alleged secrecy of the Communist activities and commitments," which is but an aggravating circumstance, but because of the activities and commitments themselves. A Communist cannot be dedicated to the search for truth since he is committed to forsake it for attending the research bespeaks the intended use of this knowledge. Now the "academic freedom" of the scientist to seek such knowledge is not at issue. What is at issue is the fact that, if he does his work in secret, he is not obligated to justify it, if challenged on moral grounds. It is irrelevant whether the example chosen is realistic or not, or what particular parts of war research happen to be done in what specific universities at this time. As long as research is done in secret, we do not know what research is done where, and why. I think a member of a university faculty has a right to know what research is being done under the auspices of his institution; not only the titles of contracts and their sources and budgets but also the content of the research, its applications and implications. I think that the fraud perpetrated by the Central Intelligence Agency on Michigan State University is a blot on that university's name, and I know personally that many faculty members of that university felt a deep shame when the unsavory role of their institution was publicly revealed.

Epilogue

The debate over the place of the military in American society will undoubtedly continue in the forseeable future. The following proposal by John Kenneth Galbraith might well serve as a focus for that debate. Unlike many critics of the military, Professor Galbraith does not believe that there is a conspiracy to the power of the military establishment or that control of the military should be wrested from the President and the Congress. To the contrary, he suggests that the growth of the influence of the military is the result of forces which can be understood and therefore controlled. What Professor Galbraith has suggested, therefore, in this statement made before a Congressional committee, a realistic program for bringing the military into a responsible relationship with the executive branch and with the Congress, each of whom share the responsibility for national defense.

John Kenneth Galbraith*

The importance of military spending in the economy—half the Federal budget, about one-tenth of the total economic product, I need not stress. Though much attention is focused upon it, this bloodless economic side is not, I venture to think, the important feature. The important feature is the peculiar constitutional and bureaucratic arrangements which govern this economic activity.

In our ordinary economic arrangements we think of the individual as instructing the market by his purchases, the market, in turn, instructing the producing firm. Thus economic life is controlled. This the textbooks celebrate. And where public expenditures are concerned, the young are still taught that the legislature reflects the will of the citizen to the Executive. The Executive, in turn, effects that will.

I have argued that with industrial development — with advanced technology, high organization, large and rigid commitments of capital — power *tends* to pass the producing organization — to the modern large corporation. Not the consumer

* The testimony of Professor Galbraith, Paul M. Warburg Professor of Economics, Harvard University, before the Subcommittee on Economy in Government Joint Economic Committee, June 3, 1969.

but General Motors tends to be the source of the original decision on the modern automobile. If the consumer is reluctant he is persuaded — to a point at least.

This part of my case has not escaped argument. Dissent raises its head everywhere these days. But where military goods are concerned one encounters little or no argument. Here, it is agreed, the historic economic and constitutional sequence *is* reversed. The citizen does not instruct the legislature and the legislature the Pentagon and its associated industries. No one wants to be that naive. Vanity becomes the ally of truth. It is agreed that the Services and the weapons manufacturers decide what they want or need. They then instruct the Congress. The Congress, led by the military bureaucrats and sycophants among its members, hastens to comply. The citizen plays no role except to pay the bill. As I say, these matters are not subject to serious dispute, those with a special capacity to believe in fairy tales apart.

The power that has brought this remarkable reversal — has assumed this authority — has, of course, been well identified. It is the military services acting individually or in association through the Department of Defense and the large military contractors. The latter, an important point, are few in number and highly specialized in the service to the military. In 1968, a hundred large firms had more than two-thirds (67.4 per cent) of all defense business. Of these, General Dynamics and Lockheed had more than the smallest fifty. A dozen firms specializing more or less completely on military business — McDonnell Douglas, General Dynamics, Lockheed, United Aircraft — together with General Electric and A.T. & T. had a third of all business. For most business firms defense business is inconsequential except as it affects prices, labor and material supply — and taxes. The common belief that all business benefits from weapons orders is quite wrong. For a few it is a rewarding source of business. The great multitude of business firms pay. The regional concentration, I might add, is equally high; in 1967 a third of all contracts went to California, New York and Texas. Ten states received two thirds. And no one should be misled by the argument that

---

* Reprinted from the Congregessional Record, June 5, 1969.

this picture is substantially altered by the distribution of sub-contracts.

One must not think of the military power — the association of the military and the defense firms — in conspiratorial terms. It reflects an intimate but largely open association based on a solid community of bureaucratic and pecuniary interest. The Services seek the weapons; the suppliers find it profitable to supply them. The factors which accord plenary power of decision to the military and the defense plants, and which exclude effective interference by the Congress and the public, are quite commonplace. Nothing devious or wicked is involved. The following are the factors which sustain the military power.

First: There is the use of fear. This, of course, is most important. Anything which relates to war, and equally to nuclear weapons and nuclear conflict, touches a deeply sensitive public nerve. This is easily played on. The technique is to say, in effect, "Give us what we ask, do as we propose, or you will be in mortal danger of nuclear annihilation." In this respect one must pause to pay tribute to Secretary of Defense Laird. He has shown himself, on this matter, to have a very high learning skill.

Second: There is the monopoly, or near monopoly, of technical and intelligence information by the Services, their suppliers and the intelligence community. This monopoly, in turn, is protected by classification. This allows the military power to exclude the lay critic, including the legislator, as uinformed. But even the best scientist can be excluded on the grounds that he is not fully informed on the latest secret technology — or does not have the latest knowledge on what the Soviets or the Chinese are up to. Here too the new Administration has been very apt. If Secretary Lard deserves a special word of commendation on the way he has learned to use fear, Under Secretary Packard must be congratulated on the speed with which he has learned to discount criticism as inadequately informed of the latest secrets.

Third: There is the role of the single-firm supplier and the negotiated contract. These are largely inevitable with high technology. One cannot let out the MIRV to competitive bidding in the manner of mules and muskets. In Fiscal 1968, as the work of this Committee has revealed, sixty per cent of defense contracts were with firms that were the sole source of supply.

Most of the remainder were awarded by negotiated bidding. Competitive bidding — 11.5 per cent of the total — was nearly negligible. With single-firm supply, and in lesser degree with negotiated supply, opposition of interest between buyer and seller disappears. The buyer is as interested in the survival and well-being of the seller as is the seller himself. No one will enter this Elysium to cut prices, offer better work, earlier deliveries or cry favoritism. That is because there is no other seller. The situation, if I may be permitted the word, is cozy.

Fourth: There is the fiction that the specialized arms contractor is separate from the Services. The one is in the public sector. The other is private enterprise. As Professor Murray Weidenbaum (the notable authority on these matters), as well as others, have pointed out, the dividing line between the Services and their specialized suppliers exists mostly in the imagination. Where a corporation does all (or nearly all) of its business with the Department of Defense; uses much plant owned by the Government; gets its working capital in the form of progress payments from the Government; does not need to worry about competitors for it is the sole source of supply; accepts extensive guidance from the Pentagon on its management; is subject to detailed rules as to its accounting; and is extensively staffed by former Service personnel, only the remarkable flexibility of the English language allows us to call it private enterprise. Yet this is not an exceptional case, but a common one. General Dynamics, Lockheed, North American-Rockwell and such are public extensions of the bureaucracy. Yet the myth that they are private allows a good deal of freedom in pressing the case for weapons, encouraging unions and politicians to do so, supporting organizations as the Air Force Association which do so, allowing executives to do so, and otherwise protecting the military power. We have an amiable arrangement by which the defense firms, though part of the public bureaucracy, are largely exempt from its political and other constraints.

Fifth: This is a more subtle point. For a long period during the fifties and sixties during which the military power was consolidating its position, military expenditures had a highly functional role in the economy. They sustained employment; they also supported, as no other expenditures do, a high technical dynamic. And there was no wholly satisfactory substitute. Hore specifically, a high federal budget, supported by the corporate and progressive personal income tax, both of which increased more than proportionally with increasing income and reduced themselves more than proportionally if income faltered, built a high element of stability into the system. And the scientific and technical character of this outlay encouraged the expansion of the educational and research plant and employed its graduates. It was long a commonplace of Keynesian economics that civilian spending, similarly supported by a progressive taxe system, would serve just as well as military spending. This argument which, alas, I have used myself on occasion was, I am now persuaded, wrong — an exercise in apologetics. Civilian spending does not evoke the same support on a large scale. (Even in these enlightened days I am told that Representative Rivers prefers naval ships to the Job Corps.) And although it is now hard to remember, the civilian pressures on the Federal budget until recent times were not extreme. Taxes were reduced in 1964 because the pressures to spend were not sufficient to offset tax collections at a high level of output — to neutralize the so-called fiscal drag. And civilian welfare spending does not support the same range of scientific and technical activities, or the related institutions, as does military spending. On a wide range of matters — electronics, air transport, computer systems, atomic energy — military appropriations paid for development costs too great or too risky to be undertaken by private firms. They served as a kind of honorary non-socialism.

Sixth and finally: There is the capacity — a notable phenomenon of our time — for organization, bureaucracy, to create its own truth — the truth that serves its purpose. The most remarkable example in recent times, of course, has been Vietnam. The achievements of bureaucratic truth here have been breathtaking. An essentially civilian conflict between the Vietnamese has been converted into an international conflict with a rich ideological portent for all mankind. South Vietnamese dictators of flagrantly repressive instincts have been converted into incipient Jeffersonians holding aloft the banners of an Asian democracy. Wholesale larceny in Saigon has become an indispensable aspect of free institutions. One of the world's most desultory and impermanent armies — with desertion rates running around 100,000 a year — was made, always potentially, into a paragon of martial vigor. Airplanes episodically bombing open acreage or dense jungle became an impenetrable barrier to men walking along the ground. An infinity of reverses, losses and defeats became victories deeply in disguise. There was nothing, or not much, that was cynical in this effort. For, for those who accept bureaucratic truh, it is the unbelievers who look confused, perverse and very wrong. Throughout the course of the war there was bitter anger in Saigon and here in Washington over the inability of numerous people — journalists, professors and others — to see military operations, the Saigon government, the pacification program, the South Vietnam army in the same rosy light as did the bureaucracy. Why couldn't all sensible people be the indignant instruments of the official belief — like Joe Alsop? (If I may pay tribute to the Edward Gibbon of the Vietcong.)

An equally spectacular set of bureaucratic truths has been created to serve the military power — and its weapons procurement. There is the military doctrine that whatever the dangers of a continued weapons race with the Soviet Union, these are less than any agreement that offers any perceptible opening for violation. Since no agreement can be watertight this largely protects the weapons industry from any effort at control. There is the belief that the conflict with communism is man's ultimate battle. Accordingly, no one would hesitate to destroy all life if communism seems seriously a threat. This belief allows acceptance of the arms race and the production of the requisite weapons no matter how dangerous. The present ideological differences between industrial systems will almost certainly look very different and possibly rather trivial from a perspective of fifty or a hundred years hence if we survive. Such thoughts are eccentric. There is also the belief that national interest is total, that of man inconsequential. So even the prospect of total death and destruction does not deter us from developing new weapons systems if some thread of national interest can be identified in the outcome. We can accept 75 million casualties if it forces the opposition to accept 150 million. We can agree with Senator Richard Russell that, if only one man and one woman are to be left on earth, they should be Americans. (Not from any particular part of the country, just Americans.) We can make it part of the case for the Manned Orbiting Laboratory (MOL) that it would maintain the American position up in space in the event of total devastation from Maine to California. Such is the power of bureaucratic truth that these things are widely accepted. And being accepted they sustain the military power.

What now should be our response? How do we get the power under control?

Our response must be in relation to the sources of power. Again for purposes of compressing this discussion, let me list specific points:

1. Everyone must know that fear is deployed as a weapon. So we must resist it. I am not a supporter of unilateral disarmament. I assume that the Soviets also have their military power sustained by its bureaucratic beliefs. But we must look at the problem calmly. We must never again be stampeded into blind voting for military budgets. These, as a practical matter, are as likely to serve the bureaucratic goals of the military power and the pecuniary goals of the contractors as they do the balance of terror with the Soviets. And we must ascertain which.

2. That part of the military budget that serves the balance of terror can be reduced only with negotiations with the Soviets. As Charles Schultze and others have pointed out, however, this is a relatively small part of the military budget. The rest serves the goals of the military power and the interests of the suppliers. This can be curtailed. But it can only be curtailed if there is a vigorous reassertion of Congressional power. Obviously this will not happen if sycophants of the military remain the final word on military appropriations. The Congress has the choice of serving the people in accordance with constitutional design or serving Senator Russell and Representative Rivers in accordance with past habit.

3. Informed technical and scientific judgment must be brought to bear on the foregoing questions. This means that the Congress must equip itself with the very best of independent scientific judgment. And the men so mobilized must not be denied access to scientific and intelligence information. I believe that on military matters there should be a panel of scientists, a Military Audit Commission, responsible only to the Congress — and not necessarily including Edward Teller — to be a source of continuing and informed advice on military needs — and equally on military non-needs.

4. We must, as grown-up people, abandon now the myth that

the big defense contractors are something separate from the public bureaucracy. They must be recognized for what they are — a part of the public establishment. Perhaps one day soon a further step should be taken. Perhaps any firm which, over a five-year period, has done more than 75% of its business with the Defense Department, should be made a full public corporation with all stock in public hands. No one will make the case that this is an assault on private enterprise. These firms are private only in the imagination. The action would ensure that such firms are held to strict standards of public responsibility in their political and other activities and expenditures. It would exclude the kind of conspiracy uncovered in the Lockheed case. It would help prevent private enrichment at public expense. In light of the recent performance of the big defense contractors, no one would wish to argue that it would detract from efficiency. And the 75% rule would encourage firms that wish to avoid nationalization to diversify into civilian production. Needless to say, the 75% rule should be applicable to the defense units of the conglomerates. Perhaps to press this reform now would direct energies from more needed tasks. Let us, however, put it on the agenda.

5. Finally, it must be recognized that the big defense budgets of the fifties were a unique response to the conditions of that time. Then there were the deep fears generated by the Cold War, the seeming unity of the Communist world, and, at least in comparison with present circumstances, the seeming lack of urgency of domestic requirements. All this has now changed. We have a wide range of tacit understandings with the Soviets; we have come to understand that the average Soviet citizen — in this respect like the average American voter — is unresponsive to the idea of nuclear annihilation. The communist world has split into quarrelling factions. I am enchanted to reflect on the Soviet staff studies of the military potential of the Czech army in case of war. Perhaps, as I have said elsewhere, we have here the explanation of their odd passion for the Egyptians. And as all philosophers of the commonplace concede, we have the terrible urgency of civilian needs — of the cities, the environment, transportation, education, housing, indeed wherever we look. It is now even agreed as to where the danger to American

democracy lies. It is from the starvation of our public services, particularly in our big cities, here at home.

Mr. Chairman, let me make one final point. Our concern here is not with inefficiency in military procurement. Nor is it with graft. These divert attention from the main point. And this is not a crusade aganst military men — against our fellow citizens in uniform. Soldiers were never meant to be commercial accessories of General Dynamics. It would horrify the great captains of American arms of past generations to discover that their successors are by way of becoming commercial accessories of Lockheed Aircraft Corporation.

The matter for concern is with the military power — a power that has passed from the public and the Congress to the Pentagon and its suppliers. And our concern is with the consequences — with the bloated budgets and bizarre bureaucratic truths that result. The point is important for it suggests that the restoration of power to the Congress is not a sectarian political hook. It is one for all who respect traditional political and constitutional processes.